THE METRE OF MACBETH

AMS PRESS
NEW YORK

THE METRE OF MACBETH

ITS RELATION TO SHAKESPEARE'S EARLIER AND LATER WORK

BY

DAVID LAURANCE CHAMBERS, A.M.

PUBLISHED BY

THE GRADUATE SCHOOL OF PRINCETON UNIVERSITY

PRINCETON
THE PRINCETON UNIVERSITY PRESS
1903

Library of Congress Cataloging in Publication Data

Chambers, David Laurance, 1879-
The metre of Macbeth.

Reprint of the 1903 ed.
Bibliography: p.
1. Shakespeare, William, 1564-1616. Macbeth.
2. Shakespeare, William, 1564-1616--Versification.
I. Title.
PR2823.C5 1972 822.3'3 78-113575
ISBN 0-404-01443-7

Reprinted from the edition of 1903, Princeton
First AMS edition published in 1972
Manufactured in the United States of America

International Standard Book Number: 0-404-01443-7

AMS PRESS INC.
NEW YORK, N. Y. 10003

CONTENTS

PREFACE.

THIS little book had its origin in a paper prepared in the spring of 1902 for a Seminar course in *Macbeth*, under the direction of Professor Thomas Marc Parrott. My design had been to present concretely a few of the metrical peculiarities of the play under discussion, and to show as briefly as possible its general place in Shakespeare's versification. But at the very threshold of investigation I found that the subject of metrical changes, which I imagined to have been worked out with scientific definiteness and completeness, was still largely a matter of dispute and conflicting testimony, that results with the most unreliable support were frequently accepted as established facts, that the tabulations which had been made were widely scattered, that the excellent work of German critics in this field was ignored by most English writers, and, finally, that *Macbeth* itself offered unexpected metrical difficulties. I became gradually involved in a series of intricate problems, and so this thesis grew far beyond the bounds of its original purpose.

It now attempts to show *when* certain metrical phenomena appeared in Shakespeare's work, *why* they appeared (as far as that can be determined), and what stage they had reached in *Macbeth*. To carry out this purpose statistics have been gathered from various sources, criticised and elaborated. In many instances only the figures for the total number of occurrences could be obtained, and these had to be converted into percentages before it was possible to base safe generalizations upon them.

The essay endeavors also to set forth, more fully than has been hitherto attempted, the metrical evidence in regard to the authorship of disputed passages in *Macbeth.*

I desire to acknowledge my great indebtedness to Professor Parrott for the illuminating suggestion and careful criticism with which he has aided me at all stages of my work, and to Dr. W. P. Woodman for his kindness in reading the proof.

DAVID LAURANCE CHAMBERS.

PRINCETON, N. J.

I.

PROSE.

The broadest possible division of a Shakespearean play is into prose and verse. Evidently the relative proportions of this division in the different dramas will not serve as a general test for their chronological arrangement, dependent as is the amount of prose upon the extent of the comic element which the author desired to introduce, and upon the number and prominence of the prose-speaking characters. Says Mr. Henry Sharpe,[1] "The time at which the plays were written does not appear to have much to do with the quantity. Roughly speaking, there is least prose in the early and late plays, and most in those in the middle as to date." In particular cases the ratio is sometimes suggestive. From the very start Shakespeare employed a liberal admixture of prose in the comedies, especially for parts of low humour.[2] In his first notable and undisputed tragedy, *Romeo and Juliet*, there is a considerable sprinkling of it. But for some reason or other (perhaps the influence of Marlowe's unvarying grandiloquence in *Edward II.*) he avoided its use in the histories until 1 *Henry IV.*[3] Later on, he extended its range of effects to include even Hamlet's imaginative discourse (*Hamlet*, II. 2. 304 ff.), though the introduction of verse in a prose-scene always marks a rise to a higher dramatic pitch, a higher emotional plane, verse being the natural language of emotion.

[1] *Transactions of the New Shakspere Society* 1880–6, p. 525.

[2] There are over 1,000 lines of prose in *Love's Labour's Lost*, spoken mainly by Sir Nathaniel, Holofernes, Dull, Costard, Moth and Jaquenetta. But the proportion varies in the comedies from *The Comedy of Errors*, one-eighth prose, to *Merry Wives*, nine-tenths prose.

[3] With the single exception of *Richard III.*, I. 4.

In *Macbeth* prose makes its appearance in four places, though only one of these (V. 1) is a "prose-scene" properly so called. In Act I., Scene 5, it is used for Macbeth's letter to his Lady; prose is the normal medium for letters, proclamations, and other written documents.[1] The Porter's rhythmical[2] speech (II. 3) is a good example of the use of prose for purposes of comedy, though, as befits the tone of the play, the jesting here is rather grim. Poor men and clowns are regularly speakers of prose in Shakespeare. Macduff, except for two lines, descends to the level of the Porter, because, as Sharpe frames the law,[3] "if an educated man who usually speaks metre meets a poor man, both speak prose." Being the language of every-day life prose contributes much to that effect of the reflux of the human world upon the fiendish which De Quincey makes the rationale of the scene. With the subsidence of the Porter and the return to serious business at the entrance of Macbeth, prose gives way to blank verse. Act IV., Scene 2, illustrates how prose lowers the dramatic pitch for the sake of emotional relief. After Lady Macduff's bitter discussion of her husband's conduct with Ross, in impassioned verse, she begins a gentle word-play with her son in prose, half-sad, half-merry. It is not, however, altogether prose. Ll. 40, 41 are surely prose, but ll. 42, 43 are as surely verse. Prose is resumed in l. 44 and thence continued as far as l. 64. This rather curious intermingling has led Professor Liddell[4] to question the genuineness of the prose parts.

[1] See Sharpe, p. 557. The only exceptions, he says, are *Titus And.*, II. 3.268 ff. ; *All's Well*, III. 4.4 ff., IV. 3.252 ff.

[2] See Dowden in *T. N. S. S.* 1874, p. 276.

[3] p. 558.

[4] Elizabethan Edition, p. 165.

He would have Lady Macduff's words in ll. 42, 43 follow immediately on l. 37, and close the dialogue, and he thinks that this excision would relieve the play of an inhuman and distorted representation of childhood. Rather it would deprive the play of a most dramatic and most Shakespearean contrast between the prattle of family life and the tragic summons to instant death. The boy is no more precocious than Shakespeare's other children, than, say, the Duke of York in *Richard III.* And, finally, this alternation of prose and verse is by no means unique. For another example see *Henry V.*, IV. 8. The arrival of the messenger with his awful tidings requires a re-heightening of the pitch and a return to verse. Messengers naturally and regularly speak in metre. In Act V., Scene I, the Doctor and the Gentlewoman discuss Lady Macbeth's mental perturbation in prose. The conversation consists of simple professional questioning and a direct report of symptoms.[1] The tone is low. It might seem strange at first sight that Shakespeare should employ prose in the sleep-walking scene which follows, where the dramatic excitement is surely intense. The attempt to explain this apparent vagary has led to some extraordinary criticism.[2] But in reality it is no vagary. Shakespeare deems prose peculiarly appropriate to the broken utterance of madness (real or assumed) in *Hamlet* and *Lear*, of frenzy in *Othello*, of intoxication in *Antony and Cleopatra*,[3] and so also of the

[1] See Delius, *Jahrbuch* V., p. 267.

[2] Hudson, for example, says: "I suspect that the matter of this scene is too sublime, too austerely grand, to admit of anything so artificial as the measured language of verse; and that the Poet, as from an instinct of genius, felt that any attempt to heighten the effect by any arts of delivery would impair it." Quoted in Furness's *Variorum*, p. 259.

[3] See *Hamlet* II. 2.171 ff., III. 1.103 ff., IV. 5.172 ff.; *Lear*, III. 4.51 ff., IV. 1.58 ff., IV. 6.131 ff.; *Othello*, IV. 1.36 ff.; *Ant. and Cleo.*, II. 7.28 ff.

irrationality of "slumbery agitation" in *Macbeth.* The pity and terror of the scene are brought out in the Doctor's blank-verse speech at the end, which, however, contrary to the general rule, indicates a falling-off in the emotional intensity. The function performed by prose in the other great tragedies—that of introducing variety in the composition—is, in *Macbeth,* largely performed by lyrical passages in a different metre.

II.

RIME.

TABLE OF RIMES.[1]

Play.	Per Cent. Heroic Lines in all Verse Lines.	Number of Heroic Lines.	Ratio Heroic to Blank Verse.	Number of Rimed Short Lines.	Songs.	Alternates.	Sonnets.	Doggerel.
Love's Labour's Lost	62.2	550	1: 1.12	66	36	242	42	187
Comedy of Errors .	19.4	216	1: 5.3	0	0	64	0	98
Merchant of Venice .	4.6	85	1:22.	34	9	4	0	2
Henry V.	3.2	62	1:30.9	2	8	0	14	0
Hamlet	2.7	64	1:36.8	8	60	81 rimes in play		
Othello	3.2	78	1:30.5	0	25	0	0	0
Lear	3.4	70	1:29.6	0	97	0	0	2
Macbeth	5.8	108	1:14.9	121	11(?)	0	0	1
Ant. and Cleo. . . .	.7	34	1:76.1	0	6	0	0	0
Winter's Tale . . .	.0	0	1:inf.	0	57	chorus: 32 rime-lines		
Tempest	.1	2	1:698.	20	50	masque: 54 rime-lines 12 song		

Of the metrical portion of the play the most comprehensive division is into rimed lines and unrimed lines, or blank verse. The percentages of the rimed

[1] The per cent. column is from König, p. 131. The rest are from Fleay's Tables in Ingleby, p. 99 ff. with some corrections. I have verified their figures for *Macbeth* and calculated the ratio column on the basis of Fleay's Figures. The eleven rimes in 1, 3, which Fleay counts as song, I should prefer to include without distinction in the short riming lines.

lines of less than five feet[1] in the different plays form no chronological criterion, as the introduction of such lines was contingent upon the character of the work Shakespeare had in hand, and very likely, too, upon the company having a popular singer.[2] It is as natural to find such rimes in *The Tempest* as in *A Midsummer-Night's Dream*. The speeches of the three weird sisters[3] are prevailingly tetrameter with a trochaic cadence, the rhythm which Shakespeare almost always, if not always, adopts in songs and in lyrical passages hardly to be told from songs. "That the individual verses do not all contain exactly the same number of syllables is obvious to the most careless reader; but the rhythmical equivalence of them never admits of doubt. The movement is as free and varied as that of popular rimes and jingles, and consequently as hard to deal with by rule-of-thumb scansion."[4] The fact that the speeches of Hecate and of the First Witch[5] are in iambic measure creates, I think, a strong presumption against their Shakespearean authorship. With the other arguments[6] impugning the genuineness of these speeches—their superfluous and incongruous character, etc.—we are not here concerned. Moreover, if Shakespeare wished to write iambics, Heaven save the foolish critic from believing that he

[1] I here include lines, themselves without rime, but in the midst of riming passages, *e. g.*, I. 3.17.

[2] See Spedding, *T. N. S. S.* 1874, p. 29.

[3] I. 1.1–7, 11, 12; I. 3.8–37; IV. 1.4–38, 44–47, 64–68, 110, 111. There are also a number of short trochaic unrimed lines of various length: I. 3.1–3, 62-69; IV. 1–3, 107–109.

[4] Manly, p. xxxii.

[5] III. 5.4–33; IV. 1.39–43, 125–132.

[6] Admirably stated by Mr. E. K. Chambers in the Arden Edition and Mr. C. H. Herford in the Eversley Edition. Mr. A. W. Verity in the Pitt Press Edition argues for the other side.

could not do so! But it remains true that for some reason or other he seldom cared to employ the four-stress iambic couplet. The only other places where it occurs—except as an occasional variation in the midst of trochaics, as in the Epilogue to *The Tempest*—are in the Gower choruses in *Pericles* (undoubtedly not by Shakespeare), and in the mock prophecy in *Lear* III. 2.81 ff. (generally regarded as an interpolation, and in any event a parody on the familiar iambic verses known as "Chaucer's Prophecy"). Many iambic lines occur in the Duke's speech in *Measure for Measure*, III. 2.275 ff., but they are so interwoven with trochaic lines that it is difficult to determine the prevailing character of the rhythm, and, moreover, this is another passage the authenticity of which has been called in question. The same may be said of "Apemantus' Grace" in *Timon*, I. 2.63 ff. Not once is the iambic tetrameter to be discovered in a passage which bears the unmistakable impress of Shakespeare's hand. *Per contra*, the *trochaic* tetrameter is found in Dumain's love-poem in *Love's Labour's Lost*, IV. 3.101–120, the songs of the fairies in *A Midsummer-Night's Dream*, the casket rimes in *The Merchant of Venice*, the verses of Orlando, Touchstone, and Phoebe in *As You Like It*, III. 2.93 ff. and IV. 3.40 ff., Tom of Bedlam's jingle in *Lear*, III. 6.69 ff., Autolycus's song in *The Winter's Tale*, IV. 4.220 ff., and the masque in *The Tempest*, IV. 1.106 ff.

What is more, the metre of these speeches of Hecate—dull, mechanical, regular, touched with favour and prettiness—is in striking and almost amusing contrast with the grotesqueness, the freedom, the bold roughness of the colloquies and incantations of the weird sisters.

Now Thomas Middleton, whose connection (direct or indirect) with *Macbeth* is indicated by the interpolation in the text of two songs from his play, *The Witch*, was fond of the iambic tetrameter. He used it, for example, in the concluding portion of one of these same songs, "Come away, come away," sung by his Hecate in III. 3; in the Raynulph choruses in *The Mayor of Queensborough*, I. 1; II. 1; IV. 2; in *The Widow*, III. 1.22 ff.; *A Chaste Maid in Cheapside*, IV. 1.162 ff.; *The Phoenix*, V. 1. 317 ff.; *The World Tost at Tennis*, second song. And that he was capable of writing as smoothly and as flatly as these Hecate speeches is proved by the following passage,[1] which, it will be noticed, concludes with a pentameter couplet exactly as in *Macbeth*, III. 5:

> "When Germany was overgrown
> With sons of peace too thickly sown,
> Several guides were chosen then,
> By destin'd lots, to lead our men;
> And they whom Fortune here withstands
> Must prove their fates in our lands.
> On these two captains fell the lot;
> But that which must not be forgot,
> Was Roxena's cunning grief;
> Who from her father, like a thief,
> Hid her best and truest tears,
> Which her lustful lover wears
> In many a stoln and wary kiss,
> Unseen of father. Maids do this,
> Yet highly scorn to be called strumpets too:
> But what they lack of't, I'll be judg'd by you."

There are several circumstances which indicate that *Macbeth* as a whole was not as successful a stage-play at first as one might imagine. But there is every reason to believe that the supernatural element made

[1] From *The Mayor of Queensborough*, I. 1.

an immediate hit. One reason for this, as Mr. Verity says,[1] is that it gave opportunity for the introduction of music. From the start, therefore, there was a tendency to impart an operatic character to the play. Incidental music has always been an important factor in its presentation.[2] This is seen in the interpolation of the songs, "Come away, come away," and "Black Spirits." And it is more than likely that it is to be seen also in these lyrical or recitative passages of Hecate and the First Witch. Middleton wrote for the King's Players (Shakespeare's old company) from 1615 to 1624. Plays were constantly being worked over by new hands for fresh presentation. It surely does not take a bold flight of fancy to imagine that the manager and actors desired some alteration in *Macbeth* to please the groundlings, and called upon Middleton to tinker with the work of the master-dramatist; and that Middleton thereupon introduced two songs and the character of Hecate[3] from *The Witch*, which he had written under the influence of *Macbeth*. And one is surely doing a service to the text of Shakespeare if one can create a presumption against the genuineness of these inferior lines.

Variations in the several plays in the ratio between the number of lines of blank verse and the number of

[1] Pitt Press Edition, p. xxxix.

[2] See Davenant's version (Furness's *Variorum*, p. 303), Pepys' interesting comment on the "divertisement" in *Macbeth*, (*Diary*, Jan. 7, 1666–7), and Fleay, *Life and Work of Shakespeare*, p. 239. There was much music in the performance of Henry Irving.

[3] It must be admitted that modern criticism has pointed out that the character of Hecate in the two plays is not the same. The Hecate of *Macbeth* is the Queen of Hell; the Hecate of *The Witch* is a mere common hag. But this is a subtlety of distinction which would not have disturbed Middleton in making his additions, especially if he was trying to write up to Shakespeare's level.

lines of rimed pentameter furnished data for the first metrical test to be applied to Shakespeare. In 1778 Malone wrote: "It is not * * * merely the use of rimes, * * * but their *frequency*, that is here urged, as a circumstance which seems to characterize and distinguish our poet's earliest performances. * * * [Shakespeare's] neglect of riming seems to have been *gradual*. As, therefore, most of his early productions are characterized by the multitude of similar terminations which they exhibit, whenever of two early pieces it is doubtful which preceded the other, I am disposed to believe, (other proofs being wanting,) that play in which the greater number of rimes is found, to have been the first composed."[1] A reference to the Table will show how Shakespeare's usage changed in this regard. In the early comedies the amount of rime is very large: in *Love's Labour's Lost* it more than balances the blank verse; in *The Comedy of Errors* there is about one rime line to every five of blank verse. By the time of the Romances, rime has all but disappeared: with the exception of the speech of Time the Chorus in *Winter's Tale*, IV. 1, there is not a pentameter couplet in the play; and in *The Tempest*, with the exception of the masque, there occurs but one tag, II. 1.326, 327.

There can be little doubt that, from the time when *Tamberlaine* (1587) first caught the popular ear with "the spacious volubility of a drumming decasyllabon" until 1640, there was "a gradual disuse of rime by every author" and "a growing dislike on the part of the public to the mixture of rime and blank verse in stage plays."[2] But it is quite another thing to say that the number of rimes in a drama will determine its exact

[1] Quoted in *T. N. S. S.* 1874, p. iv *d*.

[2] Fleay in Ingleby, p. 64. But see Nicholson in *T. N. S. S.*, 1874, p. 36.

position in the order of composition. The venerability of this test seems to have given it undue importance in the eyes of certain critics. Mr. Fleay thinks that it is the only one which "is of use *per se* for determining the chronological arrangement of Shakespeare's works,"[1] but Mr. Fleay, though an indefatigable investigator, is seldom a reliable critic. The rime-test will indeed indicate the extreme groups, but the most casual glance at the Table at the end of the essay shows that it will not decide the order of the intermediate plays. (Is one to suppose, for instance, that *Twelfth Night* was written before *Richard III*?) The reason for this fallibility may be easily demonstrated.

The operation of all the verse-tests is restricted by certain rules which are based on common sense. If these tests ever come in conflict with external evidence as to date or with the best sort of æsthetic criticism (perhaps they never do; but grant the supposition), then the verse-tests must give way. Again, one test alone is not to be taken as determinative, but all are to be compared and their relative values weighed. Thirdly, the importance of a test is in inverse ratio to the deliberateness with which the author uses the particular metrical peculiarity.[2] Those phenomena are least noteworthy which spring from a direct purpose, because this purpose may be assumed by the author for special reasons at any stage of his career. Those phenomena are most serviceable which follow a general subconscious change of taste and habit, because such a change is least arbitrary and most irrevocable. If this last law be applied to the rime-test, it is evident that its conclusions are of little worth except in setting apart the plays

[1] See *T. N. S. S.*, 1874, p. 7; Ingleby, pp. 63, 66, 67.
[2] See Spedding in *T. N. S. S.*, 1874, pp. 28–29, Nicholson in same, p. 37.

which belong in the very first division. A poet may unconsciously put down an Alexandrine or a weak ending or run on one line into the next;[1] these are matters, not of choice and purpose, but of general artistic tendency. But no man rimes unconsciously—except by accident[2] at very rare intervals, or when he does not understand the nature of rime.[3] Thought is required of most men who would write in rime, and if a playwright uses rime he has an end to be gained thereby. Down to his latest plays Shakespeare, at odd intervals, deliberately employed rime for certain definite effects. The presence or absence of such a deliberate intention must always be taken into account in the application of the rime-test.

Thus it would not be right to place *A Midsummer-Night's Dream* before *The Comedy of Errors*, simply because it contains a larger proportion of riming lines, until it had been first decided whether special incentives to rime did not exist in the case of the comedy of Fairyland; and the existence of such a long riming sequence as that put into Titania's mouth (III. 1.168–177) proves that rime here is treated with the design of producing special effects.[4] If, therefore, it is found that the proportion of riming lines in *Macbeth* is far and away above that in every play which is generally supposed to belong to the same period of authorship, it would not be right to assign it to an earlier date[5] until it has been

[1] See Dowden, *Primer*, p. 44.

[2] *Macbeth*, II. 3. 59–60, is, I think, an accidental rime. *Cf.* III. 4.99–100.

[3] *Cf.* the rimes in the *Aeneid*.

[4] See Dowden, *Primer*, p. 44; also Nicholson, *T. N. S. S.*, 1804, p. 37, who adds a remark about the plays written at the time of the poems; also König, p. 135, who thinks this the least important of the tests because the emotional pitch and the occasion must always be reckoned with.

[5] As Fleay did. See *Manual*, p. 136.

considered whether there are not special reasons for the extraordinary number of heroic couplets.

The number is really extraordinary. There are 108 lines of rimed pentameter in *Macbeth*, while *Hamlet* (twice as long) has only two-thirds as many, and *Antony and Cleopatra* (twice as long) has but one-third. In order, however, to appreciate the peculiar nature of the difficulty, it is necessary first to examine the several uses to which Shakespeare regularly puts the rimed heroic.

The couplet, then, is called upon[1]—

(1) To mark an *exit*, that the actor may not go feebly off, and that he may give an easily remembered cue to his successor. An instance of this is the familiar

Lay on, Macduff;
And damn'd be him that first cries, 'Hold, enough.' (V. 8.33 f.)

Cf. V. 7.12 f. Similarly, it indicates the disappearance of a supernatural being—which amounts to an *exit* on the stage. See IV. 1.71 f., 79 f. (also prophesies).

(2) To round off a speech of some length with a high-flown sentiment or an epigrammatic snap; *e. g.*, Duncan ends his welcome to Macbeth with the words:

Only I have left to say,
More is thy due, than more than all can pay. (I. 4.20 f.)

Cf. I. 5.70 f.; V. 3.9 f.

(3) In maxims, proverbs, old saws, and epigrams;—so Lady Macbeth's

Nought's had, all's spent
Where our desire is got without content. (III. 2.4 ff.)

Cf. I. 3.146 f. (also an aside); IV. 3.209 f.; V. 8.51 f.

(4) In asides, "which otherwise the audience might have great difficulty in knowing to be asides."[2] See

[1] See Heuser in *Jahrbuch*, XXVIII, p. 258.
[2] Abbott, *Grammar*, § 515.

I. 3.146 f. (also a proverb); I. 4.48–53;[1] V. 3.61 f. (also a tag).

(5) In the prophecies of supernatural beings. See IV. 1.90–93; *cf.* IV. 1.71 f., 79 f. Perhaps also V. 3.59 f.

(6) In moments of passionate agitation. See III. 4.135–140,[2] IV. 1.94–101.[3]

The purposes for which these couplets are used are by no means extraordinary, and parallel instances throughout could be given from other plays. The number of the couplets is extraordinary; the three long rhyming passages—I. 4.48–53; III. 4.135–140; IV. 1.94–101—are especially remarkable, and I am strongly inclined to agree with Professor Manly[4] that the last at least contains several spurious lines.

But the most striking peculiarity of the pentameter rimes in this play is the unusually large number of couplets at the end of scenes and acts.[5] Mr. Fleay says,[6] "In this play more scenes end with tags than in any other play in Shakespeare; the number of tag-rhymes is also greater than in any other play, including his very earliest." Mr. Fleay counts, in the twenty-eight scenes of *Macbeth*, twenty-one scenes ending with tags, and thirty-three rimes in all. My own reckoning,

[1] Fleay suspected this passage (*Manual*, p. 251).

[2] Apparently doubted by Fleay (*Manual*, p. 256).

[3] This, with the tags, disposes of all the pentameter rimes in *Macbeth*, except III. 5.2 f., where the couplet at the beginning of Hecate's speech counterbalances the one at the end; and II. 3.59 f., where the rime is probably accidental. IV. 1.69 rimes with a line of four-stresses, the First Witch breaking in upon Macbeth.

[4] p. 153.

[5] Abbott (§ 515) thinks this kind of couplet helped the audience to understand that the scene was finished, when the scenery was not changed, or the arrangements were so defective that the change was not easily perceptible.

[6] *Manual*, p.261.

based on a more rigorous distinction between tag-rimes and rimes used for the other purposes, gives nineteen scenes with the end-tag, and twenty-eight rimes;[1] but, though the figures are slightly reduced, the conclusions remain practically unimpaired. Compare the three Shakespearean plays which have as many scenes as *Macbeth*, or more. 3 *Henry VI* has twenty-eight scenes, ten with tags, fourteen rimes; *Antony and Cleopatra* has forty-two scenes, four with tags, six rimes; *Coriolanus* has twenty-nine scenes, two with tags, four rimes. Fifteen is the largest number of scenes which end with tags in any other play of Shakespeare's, and the play which has fifteen is the ever-puzzling *Troilus and Cressida*.

The precise nature of the singular rime problem in *Macbeth* now becomes evident and demands solution. Spedding suggested as a general explanation[2] that the actors were unwilling to have a scene end without a colophon; but this merely drives one back to the further question, why the actors developed such an acute aversion for going feebly off in 1606—a question, of course, beyond the possibility of answer. A more self-sufficient theory is offered by the Clarendon Press Editors[3] and Mr. Fleay;[4] viz., that many of the tags

[1] I. 2.64–67; I. 5.72 f. ; I. 7.81 f. ; II. 1.60 f., 63 f. ; II. 3.151 f, ; II. 4.37 f., 40 f.; III. 1. 141 f. ; III. 2.52–55 ; III. 4.142 f. ; III. 5.34 f. ; IV. 1.153 f. ; IV. 3.239 f. ; V. 1.85 f. ; V. 2.29 f.; V. 3.59–62 ; V. 4.17–20 ; V. 5.47–52 ; V. 6.7–10 ; V. 8.72–75. Note the extraordinary number in the last act.

[2] *T. N. S. S.* 1874, p. 29.

[3] Messrs. Clark and Wright, Preface, pp. ix–xii. They suspect I. 2.64–67 ; II. 1.60 f.; V. 2.29 f.; V. 5.47–50 ; V. 8.72–75. [16 lines].

[4] *Manual*, pp. 251 ff. He adds to the Clarendon Press list I. 4.48–53 (technically not a scene-tag) ; II. 3.151 f.; II. 4.37 f., 40 f.; IV. 1.153 f.; V. 3.61 f.; V. 4.17–20 ; V. 6.9 f. [22 lines]. Fleay afterwards retracted. See his *Introduction to Shakespearean Study*, p. 36.

were written, not by Shakespeare, but by another, presumably Middleton. They are certainly bald and weak enough, and their salient characteristics — unequal rhythms, faulty rimes, violent cacophany, crowding of consonants, and withal a certain "catchiness" — are Middletonian symptoms. Compare the following:

In *Macbeth*:—

(1) Our bosom interest: go pronounce his present death,
And with his former title greet Macbeth.
I'll see it done.
What he hath lost, noble Macbeth hath won. (I. 2.64–67).

(2) Which now suits with it. Whiles I threat, he lives:
Words to the heat of deeds too cold breath gives. (II. 1.60, 61).

(3) And still keep eyes upon her. So good night:
My mind she hath mated and amazed my sight. (V. 1.85, 86).

(4) Each drop of us. Or so much as it needs
To dew the sovereign flower and drown the weeds. (V. 2.29, 30).

(5) That calls upon us, by the grace of Grace
We will perform in measure, time and place:
So thanks to all at once and to each one,
Whom we invite to see us crown'd at Scone. (V. 8.72–75).

In Middleton:

(1) "Come let's away:
Of all the year this is the sportful'st day.
(*The Roaring Girl*, II. 1.430 f.)

(2) Tarry and dine here all. Brother, we've a jest,
As good as yours, to furnish out a feast.
We'll crown our table with't—Wife, brag no more
Of holding out: who most brags is most whore."
(*Ib.*, IV. 2.345 ff.)

(3) I'll take some witch's counsel for his end,
That will be sur'st: mischief is mischief's friend."
(*The Witch*, IV. 1.95 f.)

(4) " Flatters recovery now, the thing's so gross:
His disgrace grieves me more than a life's loss." (*Ib.*, V. 1.135 f.)

(5) " The worst can be but death, and let it come;
He that lives joyous, every day's his doom."
(*Women Beware Women* I. 2.232 f.)

The theory of the Middletonian authorship of the tags may be thus elaborated: The extreme brevity of *Macbeth* and the garbled state of the text of some of its scenes (notably I. 2) suggest that the play, as we have it, is a stage version reduced from the original draft. Among other alterations the revising playwright may have cut out extended passages towards the ends of various scenes and substituted rimed complets in their place.

This hypothesis gains some additional plausability from an examination of the peculiar formations of the scene-endings. Instead of a number of single tags, with a few scattering variations, such as we find in the other plays of Shakespeare, we have here almost every variety, every peculiarity. There are, in *Macbeth*, four single tags (in one of which is an Alexandrine), four double tags (in one of which there is an Alexandrine and a short line), one triple tag, three single tags followed by short lines, two double tags followed by short lines, two single tags followed by full lines, one single tag followed by a full line and a short line, one double tag with a short line between the two couplets, one double tag with a full line intervening.

It is, however, a precarious matter to lay one's finger on a line and say, "This cannot be Shakespeare's," and I would not press too closely the theory of the Middletonian tags. But whatever be the correct explanation—whether Spedding is right, or Fleay is right, or Wright is right, or all of them are wrong and the true interpreter has not yet appeared—the reader can hardly help feeling that some special and unusual influence occurred to cause this freak in *Macbeth*, and that the extraordinary number of rimed lines does not indicate for it an earlier authorship than that generally assigned.[1]

The pretty arrangements of rime-lines—interwoven quatrains, sonnets, etc.—so common in the early plays, have all disappeared long before *Macbeth*.[2] I should prefer to consider I.3.7 ("Her husband's to Aleppo gone, master o' the Tiger") as a single doggerel line, if such a thing may be, rather than to force it into a blank-verse scansion.[3] For doggerel in tragedy, *cf*. *Lear*, I. 5.55 f.

III.

BLANK VERSE.

When Milton wrote in his preface to *Paradise Lost* of "true musical delight, which consists only in apt numbers, fit quantity of syllables, and the sense variously drawn out from one verse into another," he expressed an empirical truth about the harmony of blank verse, which it had taken more than a century to demonstrate. It was not a self-evident truth to Lord Surrey, who introduced the metre about 1540:—

"There stands in sight an isle, hight Tenedon,
Rich, and of fame, while Priam's kingdom stood,
Now but a bay, and road, unsure for ship.
Hither them secretly the Greeks withdrew,
Shrouding themselves under the desert shore.
And, weening we they had been fled and gone,
And with that wind had fet the land of Greece,
Troy discharged her long continued dole."[4]

[1] A simple explanation might be developed along this line:—almost half of the tag-rimes occur in the last act; in this act there is a crowding of action, of army scenes and lively incidents; the rimes bear out the martial strain and help to impart an impressive fulness to the actors' tones.

[2] See Fleay in Ingleby, pp. 52, 53.

[3] Mr. E. K. Chambers tries to do this (Arden Edition, p. 176).

[4] Surrey's translation of the *Aeneid*, II. 29 ff.

It was not a self-evident truth to Norton and Sackville, or to Thomas Kyd, or even to Christopher Marlowe. Between the woodenness of Surrey's *Aeneid* and the extreme flexibility of *Macbeth* or *The Duchess of Malfi* is a whole world of change. As far as this general development concerns Shakespeare—and indeed he is the central figure in the movement—one may perhaps summarize it as follows:[1] Starting under a metrical bondage but little less troublesome than that of riming, he perfected himself first within the limits of the individual line, until he reached at last the utmost freedom possible within those limits; then he set himself to remove the limits, broke down the barrier at the end of the line, and proceeded to compose less and less with the single verse as a standard, and more and more in rhythmical phrases of ever-varying length; in *Cymbeline, The Winter's Tale* and *The Tempest* long familiarity leads him at times to abuse his liberty, and to write measured prose for verse. To put in it still broader terms, Shakespeare's development is a progress "in the proper adaptation of words and rhythms to the sense contained in them,"[2] a progress from a "declamatory" to a "spontaneous" verse-form.[3]

A. Stress.

Stress Modification of the Five-Foot Line. A blank-verse line is commonly defined as an unrimed line of five feet, each foot containing two syllables, and every second syllable receiving a stress or accent.

I háve | thee nót | and yét | I sée | thee stíll.[4] (II. 1.35.)

[1] See Corson, p. 61; Manly, pp. xxxiii, xxxiv.

[2] See Symonds, p. 50.

[3] Corson, p. 61.

[4] Such regular lines are most common where, as here, there is an antithesis. (Abbott, § 453 *a*.)

But this definition, like many of the definitions of our English prosody, is to be taken somewhat as a conventionalized norm, more honoured in the breach than in the observance. In the classical prosody there is a definite and unmistakable distinction between a long and a short syllable. In the English, based as it is upon an accentual and not a quantitative principle, there are many shades of gradation between an unstressed and a full-stressed syllable.[1] There is no small difference between the accent on *as* and the accent on *feeling* in the following line, and yet both count as "stress":

To feel | ing as | to sight | or art | thou but (II. 1.37.)

The modification of the norm-line by weak or intermediate stresses constitutes, therefore, one of the easiest and most frequent safeguards against monotony in blank-verse. A large majority of lines (in *Macbeth* probably 75 per cent.) have less than the whole number of five emphatic accents.[2] Out of the thirty-one lines in Macbeth's famous soliloquy (II. 1.33–64 omitting 41), to my ear only nine have five full stresses, while sixteen have four stresses, and six have but three stresses. Such results cannot be definitive, since different readers (and the same reader at different times) will emphasize differently. Nevertheless they show how preposterous is the vulgar notion that blank verse is designed to tally

[1] Mr. A. J. Ellis distinguished nine grades of force or stress: subweak, weak, superweak, submean, mean, supermean, substrong, strong and superstrong. (*Transactions of the Philological Society*, June 1876).

[2] *Cf.* Abbott (§ 453 *a*) "I should say that rather less than one of three has the full number of five emphatic accents. About two out of three have four, and one out of fifteen has three." Alden is more conservative (p. 55): "It would be safe to say that in English five-stress iambic verse, read with only the ordinary etymological and rhetorical accents twenty-five per cent. of the verses lack the full five stresses characteristic of the type."

the number of fingers on the hand. A very few lines have indeed but two strong stresses;[1] *e. g.*,

This supernátural solíciting. (I. 3.130.)

On the other hand, there are lines with more than the five primary accents, one foot bearing two. In some such cases we have a "hovering accent,"[2] where the regular word-accent and the peculiar verse-accent divide the stress between them: the accent "hovers" over two syllables; *e. g.*,

As she is troubled with thìck-còming fancies.[3] (V. 3.38).

The result is a close analogy to the classic spondee. In other cases, besides the five primary accents, a secondary accent may be found in one foot; *e. g.*,

Léad our | fìrst bát | tle; wór | thy Macdúff | and wé (V. 6.4);

or in two feet; *e. g.*,

To cry′ | Hòld, hóld! | Grèat Glá | mis wór | thy Cáwdor[4] (I. 5.55);

or even in three feet, to offset the two-stressed line; *e.g.*,

Whát hath | quènch'd thém | hath gíven | mè fíre. | Hàrk! Péace. (II. 2.2).

If the generalizations of Conrad may be accepted, despite the inadequate basis on which they rest,[5] there are more fully accentuated lines in the earliest and latest dramas than in the central plays of Shakespeare's career, more in *The Comedy of Errors* and *Macbeth* than in *The Merchant of Venice* and *Henry V.* He gives a

[1] Tennyson to the contrary. See the *Memoir* by his son, vol. II., p. 14: "In a blank verse you can have from three up to eight beats." Mr. E. K. Chambers shares this opinion. (Arden Edition, p. 174). But see Conrad in *Jahrbuch* XXXI, p. 331.

[2] See Gummere, *Handbook of Poetics*, p. 142.

[3] For other examples of hovering accent, see II. 3.150; IV. 3.28; IV. 3.196; V. 2.18; V. 3.27.

[4] For other examples of seven-stress lines, see II. 2.1,39.

[5] See *Jahrbuch* XXXI, p. 332. He deals with but four plays, and with only a thousand lines in each.

plausible explanation of this interesting circumstance by saying that in *Errors* the poet was endeavoring, after the poetic fashion of the day, to make his lines as regular as possible (therefore, with five accents); in the middle periods his allegiance to the law of regularity was shaken; and in *Macbeth* and the later plays the heavily stressed line returned with the increased fulness of expression and consequent weight of the rhythm.[1]

CONRAD'S TABLE OF STRESSES.[2]

Play	Lines with 2 stresses	3 or 4 stresses	5, 6, or 7 stresses
Comedy of Errors	6	752	202
Merchant of Venice	29	819	156
Henry V	32	814	153
Macbeth	25	734	236

Stress Modification by Change in Length of Line. Variations in stress are produced also by the addition of a whole foot to the line (resulting in an hexameter or Alexandrine[3]), or by the subtraction of one or more feet (resulting in a "short line").

When *Alexandrines* occur, the time-element has generally been obscured by the division of the line between different persons;[4] *e. g.*,

Mac. Shall be | the maws | of kites |
Lady M. What, quite | unmann'd | in folly? (III. 4.73.)

[1] For various rules about the use of stress, see Arden Edition, p. 174, and Abbott, § 453a. They deserve little attention.

[2] Based on a thousand lines in each play.

[3] Alexandrine is the regular term of art; but, properly speaking, an Alexandrine (as used in French) is a twelve-syllable line with the pause after the sixth syllable. Not all of the sixth-stress lines in Shakespeare have the pause so placed; in some respects, therefore, hexameter is the better word.

[4] Abbott, (§500) and perhaps Ellis (in Mayor p. 170) would read such a passage as two short lines rather than one long line, and call it a "trimeter couplet."

Mr. E. K. Chambers[1] thinks that the extra foot is possibly to be explained "by the second speaker breaking in on the first, so that one or two syllables are pronounced simultaneously." But it is not likely that a dramatic poet could hear the two sounds simultaneously while composing. Once in a while the Alexandrine is parceled among three speeches; *e. g.*,

Lady M. For a | few words. |
Serv. Madam,[2] | I will. |
Lady M. Nought's had, | all's spent, etc. (III. 2.4.)

On the infrequent occasions when an Alexandrine occurs in the course of a single speech, there is generally such a break in the middle of the line as to make practically two speeches instead of one.[3] Thus:

Mac. Give to the edge o' the sword
His wife, his babes, and all unfortunate souls
That trace | him in | his line.‖No boas | ting like | a fool.
(IV. 1.153.)

Or thus:

Macd. I am not treacherous.
Mal. But Macbeth is.
A good and virtuous nature may recoil
In an | imper | ial charge. ‖ But I | shall crave | your pardon.
(IV. 3.20.)

When the sense of rhythm is not disturbed in one of these ways, Alexandrines are comparatively rare. As a rule investigators of metre have shown themselves inconsistent and perplexing in their handling of this irregularity.[4] Some, like Abbott, would put every

[1] Arden Edition, p. 174.

[2] The extra foot is often a title of address, like *madam* or *sirrah*, or *my liege*, or *my lord*. It is hard to tell whether one should not count the title as altogether extra-metrical.

[3] See Arden Edition, p. 174.

[4] Thus Ellis's inconsistency is pointed out by Wagner in *Anglia* XIII., p. 356. Many of the examples which Mayor gives (pp. 161, 162) are open to a similar charge. As for Fleay, out of the fifty-six cases he counts in *Winter's Tale* (Ingleby, p. 90) I can agree to only seventeen.

apparent Alexandrine into the Procrustean bed and shorten it by drastic measures. This is to rob Shakespeare of one of the means by which he imparted variety. Others greatly exaggerate the number of instances, because they fail to consider trisyllabic feet and feminine syllables. I find at most twenty-five Alexandrines in *Macbeth; viz.*, I. 2.37 [Here the text is probably corrupt][1]; I. 2.58, 64; I. 3.111; II. 3.58, 88; III. 1.45, 46 [which I believe should be considered one line]; III. 1.139; III. 2.4, 16; III. 3.11; III. 4.73; III. 6.14, 30, 39, 49; IV. 2.30; IV. 3.8, 20, 97; V. 3.5, 37; V. 5.16, 17 [which I believe should be considered one line].[2]

As to Shakespeare's general usage, it is probably safe to accept Fleay's conclusions, *cum grano salis.* [3] Until *Twelfth Night*, the dramatist seems to have contented himself with a dozen or half-dozen Alexandrines in each play; with *Measure for Measure* the number takes a sudden leap, (revealing in this case, as in so many others, the poet's growing impatience of metrical rules), and the frequency of Alexandrines becomes a rough test for plays of the Third and Fourth Periods.

TABLE OF ALEXANDRINES.[4]

Love's Labour's Lost	4
Comedy of Errors	8
Merchant of Venice	12
Henry V	12
Hamlet	43
Othello	66
Lear	60
Macbeth	28
Antony and Cleopatra	39
Winter's Tale	56
Tempest	15

[1] *So they*, I think, belongs to the next line, from which *Doubly* should be omitted.

[2] Compare Fleay's list in Ingleby, p. 85.

[3] See Ingleby, pp. 83, 88.

[4] This Table is made from Fleay's lists in Ingleby, pp. 71–92. It does not agree in a single total with his first count (*Manual*, p. 135).

Short Lines, of one, two, three, or four measures, are much more frequent than Alexandrines, and more organically connected with the verse-structure, as definite reasons for their use can frequently be detected.[1]

(1) The defect in the line is sometimes to be pieced out by a gesture or a bit of action; *e. g.*,

> As this which now I draw. [*Drawing his dagger*]. (II. 1.41).
> This is a sorry sight. [*Looking on his hands*]. (II. 2.21).

Cf. I. 2.41; III. 3.18; III. 4.4.

(2) Sometimes the compensating pause is to be accounted for by a change in the person addressed. Macbeth says to his Lady in the banquet scene, "What man dare, I dare," and then, turning to the ghost of Banquo, "Approach thou like the rugged Russian bear." (III. 4.99). *Cf.* I. 3.126; I. 4.14; I. 7.28.

(3) Or by a change in thought. Banquo answers Macbeth's question, "Went it not so?" with "To the selfsame tune and words," and then, seeing the approach of Ross, inquires "Who's here?" (I. 3.88). *Cf.* I. 6.6;[2] II. 4.29; III. 2.51; IV. 3.28, 44.

(4) The unexpected gap may attract the attention, and so throw back upon the words of the short line an unusual emphasis. Thus, when Macbeth says that Duncan purposes to go away the next morning, Lady Macbeth replies with fearful energy,

> O, never
> Shall sun that morrow see. (I. 5.62).

Cf. III. 4.20, 51; IV. 3.219; V. 5.28 [which falls also under (8)]; V. 8.16.

(5) Accordingly, the short line is often used instead of a tag-rime or even after a tag, to give an impressive

[1] See *Jahrbuch* XXXI, pp. 335, 336; Mayor, p. 148; Arden Edition, p. 174.

[2] The text is probably corrupt here, and a word has dropped out.

ending to a scene; *e. g.*, I. 4 ends with the words of Duncan, full of dramatic irony, "It is a peerless kinsman." *Cf.* I. 3.156; IV. 2.85 [these three without tag]; I. 5.74, III. 2.56, III. 4.144, V. 2.31, V. 4.21 [these five after tag]; IV. 1.156 [after tag and an unrimed line].

(6) Or to render the *exit* of a character effective; *e. g.*, the second apparition (IV. 1.81) says

> For none of woman born
> Shall harm Macbeth. [*Descends.*]

Cf. II. 1.30; II. 3.57; V. 7.23.

(7) Short lines are frequent at the end of a speech, where a well-defined rhythm-group comes to an end. See I. 3.61, 85, 103; I. 4.43; II. 2.30;[1] II. 2.72; II. 3.25, 54, 111; III. 1.13, 18; III. 4.6, 68; IV. 2.26, 35, 43; IV. 3.17, 90, 215; V. 3.46. They appear occasionally also at the beginning of a speech, as II. 3.86; II. 4.33; III. 2.13; V. 8.23; and in broken dialogue, as I. 2.7; III. 2.26.

(8) In some cases of this sort the termination of the rhythm-group and the neglect to complete the line are occasioned by the entrance of a character; *e. g.*, II. 2.63; II. 3.68, 95, 101; III. 4.8; IV. 1.76; IV. 2.64; IV. 3.139; V. 7.4.

(9) The short line crops out, furthermore, in moments of intense emotion, when language is naturally brief, broken, and explosive. The irregular lines in the excited narrative of the battle, unless the text is corrupt, are perhaps to be explained by the breathless haste of the narrators. See I. 2.19 [I prefer to take, with the Folio, "Like valour's minion" as the short line]; I. 2.51. *Cf.* II. 3.83, 109; IV. 3.217.

[1] I prefer to take "When they did say 'God bless us!'" and "Consider it not so deeply" as two short lines, rather than as an Alexandrine with feminine syllables before the cæsura and at the end.

(10) Speaking generally, the short lines denote abruptness and lack of continuity, and so are common in questions and answers, exclamations, apostrophes, proper names, summonses, commands, etc. *Cf.* I. 2.66; II. 1.1, 10, 11; II. 2.18, 19, 30; II. 3.75; II. 4.39; III. 1.24, 29, 40; III. 2.1; III. 3.15; III. 4.13, 15, 47; IV. 1.77, 78, 143; IV, 2.80; V. 3.12, 18,34; V. 5.30.[1]

My count of the short lines in *Macbeth* is as follows. (It should be compared with Fleay's figures as given in the Table below). Total number 104.

(1) One Stress; nine instances: I. 3.103; II. 1.10, 11; II. 2.18, 19; III. 1.40; III. 3.15; III. 4.47; V. 3.29.

(2) Two Stresses; thirty instances: I. 2.19, 41, 51, 66; I. 4.14; I. 6.31; II. 1.1: II. 3.54, 68, 86, 109, 131[2]; II. 4.33, 39; III. 1.18, 24, 29; III. 4.13, 15, 20; IV. 1.143; IV. 2.26, 80, 85; IV. 3.219; V. 3.34; V. 5.30; V. 7.23; V. 8.16, 23.

(3) Three Stresses; fifty-five instances: I. 3.61, 85, 126, 156; I. 4.43, 58; I. 5.62, 74; II. 1.30, 41; II. 2.21, 30 (2), 63, 72; II. 3.57, 75, 95, 101, 111; III. 1.13; III. 2.1, 13, 26, 32, 51, 56; III. 3.18, 21; III. 4.4, 6, 8, 51, 68, 144; IV. 1.76, 77, 78, 81, 156; IV. 2.35, 43, 64; IV. 3.17, 28, 90, 139, 215; V. 2.31; V. 3.12, 18, 46; V. 4.21; V. 5.28; V. 7.4.

(4) Four stresses; ten instances: I. 2.7; I. 3.88; I. 6.6; I. 7.28; II. 1.19; II. 3.83; II. 4.29; IV. 3.44, 217; V. 8.59.

Shakespeare developed a sudden fondness for these irregular lines at the same time that he began to use the Alexandrine extensively, *viz.*, at the opening of his

[1] The so-called Amphibious Section (See Abbott, § 513, and Mayor, p. 146) is to me an Amphibious Fiction. No poet would think of composing in the way it suggests. (See Ellis in Mayor, p. 166).

[2] I prefer to take "Look to the Lady" as the short line in this passage rather than "Let's away." "Nor . . . motion" seems to me certainly a line.

Third Period.[1] Alexandrines and short lines are but particular applications of the general remark, that Shakespeare came to compose in rhythmical periods rather than in single lines. "If this be true, it may be expected that he will often end one well-defined rhythm-phrase with any of the legitimate endings, and begin the next without reference to the way in which that will affect at the junction the carrying through of a system of scansion"[2] based on the individual line; hence the long line and the short line.

TABLE OF SHORT LINES.[3]

Play.	Per Cent. of Unrimed Verse Lines.	Total Number.	1 foot.	2 feet.	3 feet.	4 feet.
Love's Labour's Lost	3.6	23	0	12	11	0
Comedy of Errors	1.4	17	2	11	4	0
Merchant of Venice	2.4	46	7	16	20	3
Henry V.	1.6	31	4	12	11	4
Hamlet	6.3	158	25	53	66	14
Othello	6.7	171	25	67	69	10
Lear	8.4	191	15	37	120	19
Macbeth	5.7	97	4	29	51	13
Antony and Cleopatra	5.2	143	11	35	71	26
Winter's Tale	2.9	58	4	14	26	14
Tempest	4.8	70	3	20	42	5

B. Substitution.

Those lines are now to be considered in which variety is secured by the substitution for the regular iambus of a trochee, or a monosyllabic foot, or a trisyllabic foot. A large number of feet are only apparently so "irregular" —if indeed we should ever apply that Johnsonian word to our "iambic licentiate." Mistakes in scansion are apt to spring from a failure to realize that many words

[1] Compare forty-two in *As You Like It* and fifty-nine in *Twelfth Night* with 108 in *Julius Caesar* and 107 in *Measure for Measure.*

[2] Manly, p. xxxiv.

[3] This Table is based on Fleay's figures in Ingleby. The per cent. column is my own.

in Shakespeare's day were not accented as they are now and that many others had not yet been frozen into a constant pronunciation. Thus we always say *persevérance*; Shakespeare always *persévérance* (see IV. 3.93). Again our practice is to say *unfélt;* Shakespeare accents either *unfélt* (*Richard III.*, I. 4.80) or *únfelt* (*Macbeth*, II. 3.142). *Cf. úndone* (I. 5.26), *únrough* (V. 2.10), *únsure* (V. 4.19). Other instances in *Macbeth* where Shakespeare's pronunciation differs from ours, or where Shakespeare's pronunciation is not consistent, are as follows:

(1) *I'nsane* (I. 3.84). This is the only time the word occurs in Shakespeare.

(2) *Authórized* (III. 4.66)—probably; *cf. Lover's Complaint*, 104, *Sonnets*, xxxv. 6.[1]

(3) *Púrveyor* (I. 6.22); only occurrence of the word.

(4) *Húmane* (III. 4.76). Both the modern words, *humane* and *human*, are always spelled *humane* in Shakespeare. Modern *humáne* is with him always *húmane*, except perhaps in *Winter's Tale*, III. 2.166.

(5) *Chástise* (I. 5.28). But *chastíse* in *Troilus and Cressida*, V. 5.4.

(6) *Hécate* (III. 5.1, etc.); always dissyllabic in Shakespeare, except in 1 *Henry VI.*, III. 2.64.[2]

(7) *Dunsínane* (IV. 1.93); elsewhere *Dúnsinane* (*e.g.*, V. 4.9.)

(8) *Cónfirm'd* (V. 8.41); so also in *Much Ado*, V. 4.17; elsewhere *confírm'd*.

(9) *Óbscure* (II. 3.64); but *obscúre* in *Venus and Adonis*, 237. Schmidt frames the following rule: Dissyllabic oxytonical adjectives and participles become paroxytonical before nouns accented on the first syllable.[3]

[1] See Browne, p. 9.

[2] Which Shakespeare probably did not write.

[3] See Appendix I. to Schmidt's *Lexicon*, Vol. II., p. 1413.

Somewhat similiar cases are the endings, *-ion*, *-ius*, *-ious*[1], and the like, the first vowel of which is now always slurred, and sometimes blended with the preceding consonant (*nation* being pronounced *nashon*), but to which Shakespeare often gave full two-syllable value, especially at the end of the line. Whether the termination is to have one or two syllables must be determined solely by the ear. Thus—

Which smoked with bloody executiön. (I. 2.18).

But

Is execution done on Cawdor? Are not (I. 4.1).

It goes without saying that in Shakespeare as in modern English poetry the *e* of the past tense or past participle in *-ed* is sometimes sonant and sometimes mute. Shakespeare at the beginning of his career was more likely to sound it than at the end.[2] I find in *Macbeth* but one[3] instance where the *e* is sounded in the past tense (*disbursèd*, I. 2.61), and ten instances where it is sounded in the participle (*drenchèd*, I. 7.68; *cursèd*, II. 1.8; *heat-oppressèd*, II. 1.39; *blessèd*, II. 3.97; *trenchèd* III. 4.27; *accursèd*, IV. 1.134; *constrainèd*, V. 4.13; *abhorrèd*, V. 7.10; *accursèd*, V. 8.17; *cursèd*, V. 8.55).

When an *r* comes next to a consonant an *e* sound may be inserted between the two letters (Compare the way Scotchmen pronounce *world*), and this *e* may be treated as part of a foot; *e. g.*,

[1] *Cf.*, also, *sergeänt* (I. 2.3).

[2] The sounding of the *-ed*, also the *-est* of the second person, and the *-eth* of the third person present are made tests by Hertzberg (*Jahrbuch* XIII, p. 257) and by Schipper (II. i. p. 295), Their observations on the *-ed* are confirmed by Conrad (*Jahrbuch* XXXI, p. 348). But the figures are few and the test is unimportant.

[3] Verbs the infinitives of which end in *d* or *t* are of course not included in this count.

Let your rememb[e]rance apply to Banquo. (III. 2.30)

Not i' the wor[e]st rank of manhood say 't. (III. 1.103)

So also *ent[e]rance* (I. 5.40), *monst[e]rous* (III. 6.8), *child[e]ren* (IV. 3.177). An anomalous instance, with *p* and an *i* sound, is *cap[i]tains* (I. 2.34), which was perhaps influenced by the French pronunciation.

Similarly long vowels or diphthongs before *r*'s in monosyllables, "since they naturally allow the voice to rest upon them, are often so emphasized as to dispense with an unaccented syllable. . . . Whether the word is dissyllabized, or merely requires a pause after it, cannot in all cases be determined[1]." As a rule I am inclined to favour the latter alternative.

What should be spoken ***here***, where our fate. (II. 3.127)

Cf. fare[2] (IV. 3.111), *fire* (IV. 1.11), *our* (I. 6.30)

On the other hand, the burr of the *r* may obscure or soften a neighbouring vowel sound, so that it is almost or quite inaudible, as—

Cleanse the stuff'd bosom of that per*i*lous stuff.[3] (V. 3.44)

The same is now and then true of other liquids (*cf. pers'nal*, I. 3.91). In the case of *evils* (IV. 3.57), *devil* (IV. 3.56, etc.), and *devilish* (IV. 3.117), either the *v* drops out, as in Scotch "de'il" and the "dram of eale,"[4] or the *i* is to be slurred.[5] Frequently, also, there are elisions in the connection of pronouns with the forms of *be* and *have*, though here again it is hard to say whether the syllable is actually dropped, or passed lightly over. See, *e. g.*, *I have* (I. 4.20), *we have* (III.

[1] Abbott, §484.

[2] Perhaps in this case the compensating pause comes before the word.

[3] See the long list in Mayor (pp. 158 ff.). The spellings *sprite* and *parlous* show the justness of this slurring.

[4] Abbott, §466.

[5] Mayor, p. 159.

3.20), *they have* (II. 1.21), *I am* (III. 1.108), *we are* (III. 1.91), etc. *God be with you* (III. 1.44) is in fact, says Walker[1], *God b' wi' you;* sometimes a trisyllable, sometimes contracted into a dissyllable;—now *good-bye.* For the rest I am inclined to think that much of the elision and slurring over which Abbott, Mayor and other investigators wax enthusiastic is imaginary,—a relic of Popean methods in metrical criticism.

I have not thought it worth while to make a count of the trochees and anapæsts in *Macbeth*, because their number is so great and their character so variable that precision would be almost impossible, and because all the practical results of such a count have been already demonstrated sufficiently by Conrad (see Table, p. 39). Trochees occur most frequently at the beginning of the line, to which they often impart an incisiveness. They are common also after the cæsura, in the third and four feet. In the second and fifth feet they are comparatively rare, because two stresses coming together without a pause make the rhythm awkward. There are many cases where two trochees occur in the same line, and an occasional instance of three. Examples:—

(1) *In the first foot:*—

Sáy to | the king | the know | ledge of | the broil. (I. 2.6)

(2) *In the second foot:*—

The eye | wínk at | the hand; | yet let | that be. (I. 4.52)

See, also, I. 3.59; I. 7.30; III. 1.97; IV. 2.71, etc.

(3) *In the third foot:*—

And his | great love, | shárp as | his spur, | hath holp him. (I. 6.23)

See, also, I. 2.67; I. 3.42, 48, 49, 58, 107, 116; II. 2.16, 59; II. 3.118; II. 4.7; III. 2.41, etc., etc.

[1] p. 227.

(4) *In the fourth foot* :—

And fan | our peop | le cold. | Nórway | himself. (I. 2.50)

See, also, I. 3.82, 86, 93, 117, 136; II. 1.32; II. 4.13; III. 1.32; III. 3.8; III. 4.2, 54, 93, 109, etc., etc.

(5) *In the fifth foot* :—

You know | not how | to do | it. Well, | sáy, sir. (V. 5.32)

See, also, IV. 2.4; V. 8.50, etc.

(6) *In the first and third feet* :—

Cánnot | be ill; | cánnot | be good: | if ill. (I. 3.131)

See, also, IV. 1.151; V. 3.49, etc.

(7) *In the first and fourth feet* :—

Ríng the | alar | um-bell. | Múrder | and treason. (II. 3.79)

See, also, I. 4.25; II. 3.124, 149; III. 1.20[1]; III. 4.49; III. 6.18, 29, 34, etc.

(8) *In the first and fifth feet* :—

Sáy, if | thou'dst ra | ther hear | it from | oúr mouths. (IV. 1.62)

(9) *In the third and fourth feet* :—

No less | to have | dóne so: | lét me | infold thee. (I. 4.31)

(10) *In the fourth and fifth feet* :—

But in | it shares | some woe, | thoúgh the | máin part. (IV. 3.198)

See, also, IV. 3.18.

(11) *In the first, second, and third feet* :—

Ay′, and | sínce too, | múrders | have been | perform'd. (III. 4.77)

See, also, V. 6.4.

(12) *In the second, fourth, and fifth feet* :—

What a haste | lóoks through | his eyes! | Só should | hé look. (I. 2.46).

Trisyllabic feet, or anapæsts, are not at all unusual, and are generally felt to add speed to the rhythm.

In my | volup | tuousness: | your wives, | your daughters. (IV. 3.61)

All con | tinent | impe | diments would | o'erbear. (IV. 3.64)

[1] Read as one line with 19.

What a haste | looks through | his eyes! | So should | he look. I. 2.46)

That look | not like | the inha | bitants | o' the earth. (I. 3.41)

Monosyllabic feet are comparatively rare, appearing only when the stress upon the single syllable is very heavy, or the quantity of the syllable is very long, or a pause makes up for the omission of the light syllable. "Initial truncation" (*i. e.* the dropping of the first light syllable of the line,) so common in other English iambic rhythms, is especially rare in Shakespearean blank verse. I think that I detect an instance of it in I. 2.45.

Who | comes here? | The wor | thy thane | of Ross.[1]

Other examples of monosyllabic feet are I. 2.5 (fourth foot), I. 4.35 (fourth foot), I. 5.41 (fourth foot), I. 5.58 (fifth foot), II. 1.51 (third foot), III. 4.133 (third foot), III. 6.14 (fourth foot), IV. 1.22 (third foot).

As Shakespeare's verse grows freer and bolder, more in harmony with the thought and the emotion, it is only to be expected that these irregular feet should become more and more frequent with him.

TABLE OF SUBSTITUTIONS.[2]

Play	Trochees	Anapæsts	Monosyllabic feet	Total
Comedy of Errors	260	1	2	263
Merchant of Venice	215	2	0	217
Henry V..	261	4	1	266
Macbeth	309	11	6	326

Conrad's special Table of Trochees presents some interesting matter:—

Play	Total	At Beginning	After Cæsura	2 in a line	3 in a line
Comedy of Errors .	260	185	32	12	0
Merchant of Venice	215	135	44	15	0
Henry V.	261	164	61	24	0
Macbeth	309	149	102	29	5

[1] So Verity (p. 271). *Cf. Measure for Measure*, V. 1.315, *Richard II.* I. 1.20.

[2] From Conrad's Tables, in *Jahrbuch* XXXI, pp. 350–352, which are based upon a thousand lines in each play.

In the trochees at the beginning of the line, he says, we have the striking phenomenon that *Henry V.* as well as *Macbeth* falls behind *Errors*, a fact which is best explained by the increased overflowing of the verses; the *enjambement* would be obscured if a stressed end-syllable of one line were followed by a first syllable of the next also accented. On the other hand, the trochees after the cæsura form a steadily rising column in the four plays, which shows that in the later dramas the cæsura becomes more and more the principal pause. If you omit the trochees which are least felt (*i. e.*, those at the beginning), you have this steady progression: *Errors*, 75; *Mer. of Ven.*, 80; *Henry V.*, 97; *Macbeth*, 160. What was not clear in the sum total of the trochees we recognize clearly here, *viz.*, that the use of the trochee as a rhythmical counterstroke grew with the years; that, therefore, with the trochees, too, the same evidence is before us as with the anapæsts and the monosyllabic feet.

C. Feminine Syllables.

However the poet might diversify the internal structure of the line, there was always a strongly stressed end-syllable, against which he must come with a jolt every minute. The ring of that end-syllable in his mind (long associated with the enforcement of rime) was a constant temptation to "bumbast out" the blank verse with unnecessary phrases, repetitions and plays on words.[1] We must now consider by what devices Shakespeare overcame this champion of dulness, this chief foe of liberty and variety.

One thing he did was to add an unstressed syllable

[1] As in *Richard III.*, II. 2.71-79, *Love's Labour's Lost*, III. 1.196, 197. ee Corson, p. 54.

after the last accent, which was thus modified by a "kind of grace-note[1]," *e. g.*,

He hath a wisdom that doth guide his val(our.[2] (III. 1.53.)

By an extension of the peculiarity we sometimes have two such extra syllables:

My thought, whose murder yet is but fantas(tical. (I. 3.139.)

The extra syllable may even appear at the end of an Alexandrine:

The sleepers of the house? speak, speak! O gentle la(dy. (II. 3.88.)

That the comparative frequency of these "feminine endings," as they are called, indicates, in a general way, the date of a play was first pointed out by Charles Bathurst in his classic work on Shakespeare's versification (1857).[3] Stating the fact broadly, if the feminine endings are few we may infer that the play is of early composition; if they are numerous, that the play belongs to the period of mature authorship.

Compare two typical passages, in each of which a woman scolds a man. The first is from an early play, *The Comedy of Errors*, II. 2.112-120:

[1] Dowden, p. 43.

[2] Abbott says (§455) that 'the extra syllable is very rarely a monosyllable, still more rarely an emphatic monosyllable.' Only the latter part of this statement is true. Unemphatic monosyllables are common enough as feminine endings. Fletcher will use even an emphatic and important word after the final stress. See Symonds, p. 35.

[3] See Bathurst, pp. 3, 147, 149. Roderick (See *T. N. S. S.* 1874, Appendix, p. 66) first noticed the peculiarity in his remarks on *Henry VIII.*, which were printed in Thomas Edwards' *Canons of Criticism* (1758). Malone quoted Roderick (See *T. N. S. S.* 1874, p. 443), but seemed, poor man, to be doubtful of the fact! S. Hickson (in *The Westminister and Foreign Quarterly Review*, No. XCII, and No. LXXVII., for April 1847; reprinted in *T. N. S. S.* 1874, Appendix, p. 25), and James Spedding (in *The Gentleman's Magazine* for August 1850; reprinted in the same volume, Appendix, p. 1) used this test for separating Shakespeare's and Fletcher's parts in *The Two Noble Kinsmen* and *Henry VIII.*, respectively. This was the first test to be used with arithmetical precision (Spedding, p. 14), and to be so applied to all the plays (Hertzberg, in *Jahrbuch* XIII, p. 252).

Ay, ay, Antipholus, look strange and frown:
Some other mistress hath thy sweet aspects;
I am not Adriana nor thy wife.
The time was once when thou unurged wouldst vow
That never words were music to thine ear,
That never object pleasing to thine eye,
That never touch were welcome to thy hand,
That never meat sweet-savour'd in thy taste,
Unless I spake, or look'd, or touch'd, or carved to thee.

In all the forty-line speech of Adriana from which this is quoted there are but two feminine endings (ll. 121, 141). Compare with this Paulina's speech in *The Winter's Tale*, III. 2. 184–193:—

For all
Thy by-gone fooleries were but spices of(it.
That thou betray'dst Polixenes, 'twas noth(ing;
That did but show thee, of a fool, incon(stant
And damnable ingrateful: nor was't much
Thou wouldst have poison'd good Camillo's hon(our,
To have him kill a king; poor trespasses,
More monstrous standing by: whereof I rec(kon
The casting forth to crows thy baby-daugh(ter
To be or none or little.

I count in all 429 feminine endings in *Macbeth*, or 26. 9% of the blank-verse lines. The results of König and Fleay are approximately the same. Of these 429, fourteen are triple endings, *viz*, I. 3.129, 139; I. 4.26; I. 5.49; II. 1.3; II. 3.114, 120: II. 4.10; III. 1.81; III, 2.11; III. 4.2, 37; IV. 3.66; V. 4.6. Moreover, thirty-four of the short lines end with a feminine syllable.

It will be observed from the Table that the feminine endings are only an approximate chronological test, and that the percentages do not form a steadily rising column. After 1599, Shakespeare appears always to have employed at least one feminine ending to every five lines; towards the conclusion of his career he used as many as one in three; and, beginning with *Macbeth*

TABLE OF FEMININE ENDINGS.[1]

Plays	Total (Fleay)	% (König)	% (Fleay)	% (Hertzberg)
Love's Labour's Lost	26	7.7	4.	4.
Comedy of Errors . .	178	16.6	15.4	12.
Merchant of Venice.	325	17.7	17.4	15.
Henry V.	336	20.5	17.5	18.37
Hamlet	528	22.6	22.4	25.
Othello	679	28.1	28.5	26.
Lear	580	28.5	28.	27.36
Macbeth	420	26.3	26.3	23.47
Ant. and Cleo. . . .	666	26.5	25.7	26.
Winter's Tale. . . .	675	32.9	34.7	32.5
Tempest	472	35.4	34.	32.

and omitting the three plays of mixed authorship, *Timon*, *Pericles* and *Henry VIII.*, the increase of the feminine endings does in fact follow the precise order of the last six dramas.[2] Before 1599, however, the plays exhibit the most surprising divigations from a uniform progression, the poet's unconscious attitude toward the end-syllable seeming to alter with each new composition. These variations are, doubtless, in many instances to be connected with variations in the amount of rime. There are comparatively few double rimes in English, and so when the dramatic poet is making frequent use of the couplet, his blank verse will feel the influence. Many rimes imply few feminine endings, and *vice versa*.[3]

Feminine endings never became with Shakespeare a mere matter of formal and deliberate adoption, even though in *The Tempest* and *The Winter's Tale* they are

[1] In this Table the first (or total) column is from Fleay's Tables in Ingleby ; the second is from König, p. 132 ; the fourth from *Jahrbuch* XIII, p. 252. I take König's list of percentages to be the most accurate ; note the general parallelism between his list and that which I have figured out from Fleay's totals (third column). See what Fleay says about Hertzberg in Ingleby, p. 58.

[2] That is, if one follows König.

[3] Compare *Love's Labour's Lost* and *Midsummer-Night's Dream* with *Comedy of Errors* and *Richard III.*

almost the normal rhythm. With Fletcher, on the other hand, they are a distinguishing mannerism.[1] Through page after page he voluntarily substitutes for the standard decasyllables lines with one, two, and three extra end-syllables,[2] and so imparts to his verse a languorous, luxurious retardation, surfeiting by its sweetness, and fatiguing by its monotony. But Shakespeare's versification is the least mannered of all poets; it is evolved from an inner law of harmony and is always thoroughly organic. When Shakespeare used feminine endings it was not because he thought them an adornment, but because his "feeling instinctively reached out for them"[3] at moments when they would give a desirable effect. Consequently the feminine endings are unevenly distributed among the scenes of the same play.

With the aid of critical *dicta* supplied by Abbott and Mayor[4] I have determined in *Macbeth* some of the peculiar effects produced by a multiplication of feminine endings. Often, of course, their influence, though felt, is too vague to be expressed in precise words, but at times it becomes a definite and definable quantity.

(a.) Lines are appropriately feminine in the polite and graceful conversation of society. The place in *Macbeth* where the feminine endings are most numerous is the dialogue between Duncan and his hostess on the arrival of the court at Inverness. (I. 6.10-31.)

Duncan. See, see, our honour'd hostess!
The love that follows us sometime is our trouble,
Which still we thank as love. Herein I teach you
How you shall bid God 'ild us for your pains,
And thank us for your trouble.

[1] See G. C. Macaulay, *Francis Beaumont*, pp. 43, 44; J. A. Symonds pp. 34ff.

[2] See Alden, p. 226.

[3] Corson, p. 78.

[4] Abbott in *T. N. S. S.* 1874, p. 75; Mayor, 175.

Lady Macbeth. All our service
In every point twice done, and then done double,
Were poor and single business to contend
Against those honours deep and broad wherewith
Your majesty loads our house: for those of old,
And the late dignities heap'd up to them,
We rest your hermits.
Duncan. Where's the thane of Cawdor?
We coursed him at the heels, and had a purpose
To be his purveyor: but he rides well;
And his great love, sharp as his spur, hath holp him
To his home before us. Fair and noble hostess,
We are your guests to-night.
Lady Macbeth. Your servants ever
Have theirs, themselves, and what is theirs, in compt,
To make their audit at your highness' pleasure,
Still to return your own.
Duncan. Give me your hand;
Conduct me to mine host: we love him highly,
And shall continue our graces towards him.
By your leave, hostess.

Here in twenty-two lines there are fourteen feminine endings. The straining after excessive courtesy voices itself in the lingering grace of the feminine rhythm. Perhaps this is the reason why Fletcher, preëminently the poet of society, is so fond of it.[1]

(b). In moments of excitement, when most of the rules are disregarded, the extra end-syllable naturally makes its appearance. In the broken frenzy of Macbeth's address to the ghost (III. 4.100–106) there are three feminine endings; compare with this the subdued reflectiveness of ll. 75-82 in the same scene, where there are none.

(c). On the other hand the feminine ending is rare

[1] The long-drawn-out effect of Fletcher's lines is due partly to the fact that a large per cent. of his feminine-ending verses are end-stopped. Contrast in this respect Shakespeare's practice. (See Browne, p. 21.)

when the conversation is familiar, when there is an extended narrative, or when the poet permits himself a full flight of pure poetry,—that is, when the regular verse-form would readily flow from the pen. For examples, see Lennox's speech in III. 6.1-23, two feminine endings, both proper names; Ross's report to Macbeth in I. 3.89–99, no feminine endings. In Act I., Scene 2, where the Sergeant and Ross narrate the fortunes of the fight, the feminine endings average less than one in five. There is no precise counterpart in *Macbeth* to Mercutio's Queen Mab speech or Horatio's "A mote it is to trouble the mind's eye" (*Hamlet*, I.1.112 ff.), the instances cited by Mayor and Abbott for poetic regularity.

(d). In soliloquies that are quietly meditative, hendecasyllabics are infrequent [*cf.*, *e. g.*, Macbeth's "sear and yellow leaf" soliloquy, V. 3.20–28, one feminine ending], but when the throught is agitated or vehemently argumentative, they are prevalent. This is strikingly illustrated by the soliloquy in I. 7.1–28. The first eighteen lines have seven double endings, because Macbeth is in feverish debate with himself; then comes the trumpet-tongued outburst of poetry, with the return of a feminine ending (l. 26), only after Macbeth has returned to self-examination. See also I. 5.16-31: the first eleven lines express the acme of excitement, and of them six lines end femininely; the last five develop a single poetic idea and are perfectly regular. In II. 1.33–64, the feminine endings are most rare in the poetic passage beginning "Now o'er the one half-world" (ll. 49-60); in III. 1.48-72, they are most rare in the poetic passage beginning "Then prophet-like" (ll. 59-72). These cases are enough to establish the point beyond doubt.

One rises, therefore, from a study of the feminine endings with renewed reverence for the minute perfection of Shakespeare's art and renewed faith in the organic character of his verse. One feels that he called upon this device with reason, for the sake of dramatic[1] variety, and called upon it increasingly with the years, as his instinct became unshackled and unerring.

Corresponding to the feminine ending, there may be one or two light syllables added before the cæsural pause. These syllables might, of course, be counted as parts of trisyllabic feet,[2] but the analogy between the terminal pause and the internal pause of the line, especially when Shakespeare was composing, not by the single verse, but in rhythmical paragraphs, leads one rather to consider them as extra, or feminine, syllables.

One syllable :

Wake Duncan with thy knock(ing ! ‖ I would thou couldst! (II. 2.74.)

But mine own safe(ties. ‖ You may be rightly just. (IV. 3.30.)

Two syllables:

Contending 'gainst obed(ience, ‖ as they would make. (II. 4.17.)

In restless ec(stasy. ‖ Duncan is in his grave. (III. 2.22.)

In an Alexandrine:

Like syllable of dol(our. ‖ What I believe, I'll wail. (IV. 3.8.

Combined with feminine ending:

The thane of Caw(dor, ‖ began a dismal con(flict. (I. 2.53)

The air is del(icate. ‖ See, see, our honour'd hos(tess! (I. 6.10)

[1] I say "dramatic" rather than "poetic". Bathurst (p. 148) notes that feminine endings are very rare in Cowper and Milton; Mayor's Tables (p. 186) show that the same is true for the non-dramatic works of Tennyson. But they are more numerous in *Samson Agonistes* than in *Paradise Lost*, and in *Queen Mary* than in *Idylls of the King*. (See Alden, p. 233). They are characteristic of epic rather than dramatic blank verse.

[2] See the debate on this point between Ellis and Mayor, in Mayor, pp. 153, 168, 178.

I count in all eighty-nine cases of the feminine cæsura; of these, there are eight which have two syllables, *viz.*, in addition to the the three examples cited above, III. 1.80, III. 4.121, IV. 1.89, IV. 3.239.[1] Twenty-eight lines have feminine syllables both at the cæsura and at the end.

The comparative frequency of these mid-line extra-syllables has been made a verse-test by Fleay, and seems to separate effectively the plays of the Second Period from those of the Third.[2]

TABLE OF FEMININE CÆSURAL SYLLABLES.

Play	Number of Syllables	Play	Number of Syllables	Play	Number of Syllables
Love's Lab. Lost	0	Hamlet	78	Ant. and Cleo.	120
Com. of Errors .	0	Othello	208	Winter's Tale.	60
Mer. of Ven. . .	32	Lear	131	Tempest	33
Henry V. . . .	25	Macbeth[3]	78		

D. End-Stopped and Run-On Lines.

After all the feminine syllables do not remove the real difficulty of the troublesome emphatic ending of the line, because they do not of themselves relieve the final pause. Probably the most important of all the changes which worked themselves out in Shakespeare's metrical habit was the decrease of end-stopped lines. A line is said to be "end-stopped," when the voice naturally rests at its conclusion.

The presence of the pause is not necessarily indi-

[1] See Wagner, in *Anglia* XIII., p. 357.

[2] Contrast twenty-two in *As You Like It*, twenty-eight in *Twelfth Night*, thirty-five in *Julius Caesar*, with ninety-eight in *Measure for Measure*, and 208 in *Othello*.

[3] One reason why my count of these syllables yields a larger result than Fleay's is the fact that several lines which he reckons Alexandrines I analyze in this manner.

cated by a punctuation mark[1]; it is sufficient for the purpose that the last word should be dwelt upon; the pause may be rhetorical, rather than strictly grammatical.[2] Thus, I. 3.141 is an end-stopped line:—

> Is smother'd in surmise, and nothing is
> But what is not.

A line is said to be "run-on," when the sense and the voice are carried forward without a pause into the line that follows.

The alteration in Shakespeare's manner with regard to *enjambement* can be best disclosed by the juxtaposition of passages from an early and a late play. *King John* will furnish an example of the youthful end-stopping:—

> Thou shalt be punish'd for thus frighting me,
> For I am sick and capable of fears,
> Oppress'd with wrongs and therefore full of fears,
> A widow, husbandless, subject to fears,
> A woman, naturally born to fears;
> And though thou now confess thou didst but jest,
> With my vex'd spirits I cannot take a truce,
> But they will quake and tremble all this day.
> What doest thou mean by shaking of thy head?
> Why dost thou look so sadly on my son?
> What means that hand upon that breast of thine?
> Why holds thine eye that lamentable rheum,
> Like a proud river peering o'er his bounds?
> Be these sad signs confirmers of thy words?
> Then speak again; not all thy former tale,
> But this one word, whether thy tale be true.
>
> (III. 1.11-26.)

One feels in reading lines like these that the poet

[1] See Seccombe and Allen, *The Age of Shakespeare*, Vol. II., p. 113.

[2] An attempt was made by the Tests Committee of the St. Petersburg Shakespeare Circle (*Engl. Stud.* III, p. 473) to substitute a purely grammatical test for the phonetic one hitherto used, but the attempt was hardly successful. See König's comments, p. 109, footnote.

was saying not altogether what he would, but what he could. A passage from *Macbeth* will illustrate the gain in rapidity, variety, vivacity, and ease, which accompanied the increase of *enjambement*.

> Macduff, this noble passion,
> Child of integrity, hath from my soul
> Wiped the black scruples, reconciled my thoughts
> To thy good truth and honour. Devilish Macbeth
> By many of these trains hath sought to win me
> Into his power, and modest wisdom plucks me
> From over-credulous haste: but God above
> Deal between thee and me! for even now
> I put myself to thy direction, and
> Unspeak mine own detraction, here abjure
> The taints and blames I laid upon myself,
> For strangers to my nature. I am yet
> Unknown to woman, never was forsworn,
> Scarcely have coveted what was mine own,
> At no time broke my faith, would not betray
> The devil to his fellow and delight
> No less in truth than life: my first false speaking
> Was this upon myself.
>
> (IV. 3.114-131.)

It is commonly stated[1] that the progression of *enjambement* in the several plays, indicating as it does an indeliberate change of habit, and not, like rime, depending upon voluntary choice, is the most regularly continuous of all the progressions, and that, therefore, the *enjambement*-test is the most valuable. Accordingly I expected to find here, upon investigation, chronological evidence nearly, if not perfectly, conclusive. I was disappointed. The *enjambement*-test may, indeed, be better fitted than the others for general application to Shakespeare's whole career, but it serves only to in-

[1] See *e. g.*, Dowden, p. 39; Furnivall in *T. N. S. S.* 1874, p. 31 (footnote); Ingram, same vol., p. 455; Bathurst, p. 2; König, p. 135.

dicate groups, not the order of plays within the groups. Two counts of the run-on lines have been made. One was accomplished by Dr. Furnivall, whose name is identified with this test because of the prominence to which he raised it[1]; but Furnivall counted only eight plays[2], and committed the palpable mistake of including rime-lines in his ratios.[3] *Enjambement* in the couplet is a very different thing from *enjambement* in blank verse, much more difficult and infrequent.[4] The other count, made by König for all the dramas, bases scientific results upon a loose æsthetic distinction[5], but I accept his figures as consistent and consistency is the main point in such matters. My own reckoning of the run-on lines in *Macbeth* yields a total considerably less than his, *viz.* 470, or 29.4 % of the blank-verse lines; but

[1] It was first noticed by Malone (1778), and was worked out with ingenuity by Bathurst (1857). See p. 2 of his delightful little book, and the remarks on the several plays.

[2] *Viz.*, *Love's Labour's Lost*, *Comedy of Errors*, *Two Gentlemen*, *Tempest*, *Cymbeline*, *Winter's Tale* (See Leopold Shakspere, p. xx; König, p. 133), *Henry VIII.* (*T. N. S. S.* 1874, app., p. 24) and *Two Noble Kinsmen* (*ib.*, p. 65).

[3] See König, p. 133 (footnote); Fleay in Ingleby, p. 60, Rule 3.

[4] See Alden, pp. 184 ff., 437 ff.

[5] This distinction is drawn on p. 109. It is between the mild *enjambement* which makes allowance for the verse in its rhythmical signification, and the rough *enjambement* whicn overflows the metrical pause. Thus, in I. 4.22, 23,—

> The service and the loyalty I owe,
> In doing it, pays itself. Your highness' part
> Is to receive our duties;—

the first line has the mild *enjambement*, the second has the rough. It is only the latter (generally corresponding with Furnivall's "run-on line") for which Shakespeare shows diminishing aversion, and which, therefore, is chronologically determinative. But König would include in the latter class lines like III. 1.126 and III. 4.43, where the pauses after *lord* and *sir* surely make the lines end-stopped.

my definition of the term "run-on" is more narrow and rigorous.

TABLE OF RUN-ON LINES.[1]

Play	Per Cent. of Blank Verse	Per Cent. of Verse-Lines
Love's Labour's Lost	18.4	5.2
Comedy of Errors	12.9	8.5
Merchant of Venice	21.5	
Henry V.	21.8	
Hamlet	23.1	
Othello	19.5	
Lear	29.3	
Macbeth	36.6	
Antony and Cleopatra	43.3	
Winter's Tale	37.5	32.
Tempest	41.5	24.8

According to König's figures Shakespeare's use of the unstopped line took a jump with *Lear* (of 9.8 %,) another with *Macbeth* (of 7.3 %), and still another with *Antony and Cleopatra* (of 6.7 %). He was rapidly breaking away from the confinement of end-pauses, because with a large majority of end-stopped lines he could not make narrative fluent or conversation rapid. Yet an over-abundance of run-on lines perhaps makes the phrasing too intricate, the rhythm too prosaic, for very deep and active tragedy.[2] The prevalence of such lines is one of the distinguishing

[1] The first column is from König, p. 133 ; the second is from Furnivall (Leopold Shakspere, p. xx), the figures having been converted from ratios to per cents.

[2] Perhaps one ought to comment here upon the fact that not only does the total number of stopped lines fall off, but also the use of many of them in succession. König (p. 105) cites *Two Gentlemen*, IV. 4.184-210 (twenty-seven lines, one *enjambement*), *King John*, III. 1.8-39, and *Julius Caesar*, I. 2.138-158. Later such a long chain of stopped lines is to be found only in *Pericles*, I. 2.1-47 and *Henry VIII.*, II. 1.55-79, both suspected passages. Conversely, in the youthful dramas we have at most five successive run-on lines, and that in but two instances (1 *Henry VI*, IV. 4.2-6, *Romeo and Juliet*, II. 6.24-28), while in *Macbeth* we have two passages of seven in succession (III. 6.42-48, IV. 3.1-7) and one of nine (IV. 3.115-123), and later plays have still more extended sequences.

characteristics of Shakespeare's Fourth Period, the period of the Romances.

E. Light and Weak Endings

The most insistent metrical reason for a Fourth Period, however, is the sweeping introduction in these last plays of weak *monosyllabic* endings. Indeed, so numerous and characteristic do they grow that the period may best take its designation from them as the "Weak-Ending Period." The word "weak" is generic, covering two degrees of enfeeblement. On some of the final monosyllables "the voice *can* to a certain small extent dwell."[1] They are therefore termed "light" endings. To this class belong the pronouns *I*, *thou*, *you*, *he*, *she*, *we*, and *they*, the auxiliaries *do*, *has*, *shall*, *may*, *can*, and the like, the verbal forms *am*, *be*, etc., the relatives *who*, *which*, *what*, etc., and a few other words.[2] For example,—

> If I say sooth, I must report they were
> As cannons overcharged with double cracks. (I. 2.36)

There are twenty other cases of light endings in *Macbeth*, as follows: *upon*[3] (I. 4.37), *be* (I. 5.16), *been* (I. 7.17), *would* (I. 7.50), *upon* (I. 7.69), *upon* (I. 7.70), *but* (II. 1.37), *been* (III. 1.78), *what* (III. 1.110), *could* (III. 1.118), *he* (III. 6.38), *might* (III. 6.43), *be* (IV. 1.147), *been* (IV. 3.67), *may* (IV. 3.70), *be* (IV. 3.73), *such* (IV. 3.77), *been* IV. 3.86), *should* (IV. 3.97), *hath* (IV. 3.189).

But the "weak" endings *par excellence* are those which "are so essentially *proclitic* in their character (to use a term applied by Hertzberg in dealing with this

[1] See Ingram, in *T. N. S. S.* 1874, p. 447.

[2] Ingram counts fifty-four light monosyllables, to which the Tests Committee of the St. Petersburg Shakespeare Circle (*Engl. Stud.* III., p. 483) would add forty.

[3] This dissyllable is added to the list of monosyllables.

subject) that we are forced to run them, in pronunciation no less than in sense, into the closest connection with the opening words of the succeeding line"[1]. These winged words embrace monosyllabic prepositions (*e. g.*, *at*, *by*, *for*, *from*, *in*, *of*, *on*, *to*, *with*) and conjunctions (*e. g.*, *and*, *as*, *but*, *if*, *nor*, *or*, *than*, *that*).[2] Two such weak endings are commonly reckoned in *Macbeth*:

> He hath been in unusual pleasure, and
> Sent forth great largess to your offices. (II. 1.13.)

(Here the Folio reads *pleasure*, *And sent*; Jennens made the correction in the lineation.)

> I put myself to thy direction, and
> Unspeak mine own detraction. (IV. 3.122.)

It is possible, as Professor Parrott has pointed out to me, that a change similar to the one made by Jennens should be adopted in V. 7.22, where otherwise the pause after *bruited* would have to make up for the omission of a stressed and an unstressed syllable. The rhythm of both this line and the next is certainly improved if the *And* is transferred.

> Seems bruited. Let me find him, fortune! and
> More I beg not.

Professor Ingram[3] distinguished the two groups in

[1] Ingram, p. 447; also *Jahrbuch* XIII., p. 253.

[2] The St. Petersburg Committee (p. 484) try again to substitute a purely grammatical test, and to make up a complete list of all possible weak endings. They add to Ingram's list (See p. 501) *both*, *down*, *else*, *are*, *hence*, *lest*, *like*, *near*, *next*, *nigh*, *off*, *out*, *round*, *save*, *since*, *sith*, *so*, *still*, *thence*, *through*, *whilst*, *while*, *up*, *yet*. On the whole they have failed again, because their rules lead to a total disregard of the important element of quantity. (See König, p. 100, footnote, and Schipper, II. i., p. 291.) This criticism applies also to their additional list of light endings. Some of their points (*e. g.*, 4 and 8 on p. 485) seem well taken.

[3] To whom we owe the final elaboration of the test. The weak endings were first noticed as a mark of the later plays by Bathurst (p. 3; also p. 104). The two degrees were discriminated by Craik (p. 39), who also excellently described their effect on the verse (pp. 36, 37). Spedding first insisted upon the necessity of counting the weak endings. (*T. N. S. S.* 1874, p. 31.)

this way: he looked through Milton's two epics and Wordsworth's *Excursion* to see what words of this general character they allowed at the ends of their lines. Such he made the "light" endings, because he knew that the grave non-dramatic verse of these poets would never approach "the extreme of the proclitic structure".

With the introduction of weak endings the death blow is dealt to the emphatic close of the line. The force of freedom could no further go.

TABLE OF LIGHT AND WEAK ENDINGS.[1]

Plays	Number of Light	Number of Weak	Per Cent. of Light	Per Cent. of Weak	Per Cent. Both of
Love's Labour's Lost	3	0	.48	.00	.48
Comedy of Errors . .	0	0	.00	.00	.00
Merchant of Venice .	6	1	.32	.05	.37
Henry V.	2	0	.10	.00	.10
Hamlet.	8	0	.34	.00	.34
Othello	2	0	.08	.00	.08
Lear	5	1	.24	.04	.28
Macbeth	21	2	1.30	.12	1.42
Ant. and Cleo. . . .	71	28	2.74	1.08	3.82
Winter's Tale	57	43	2.92	2.21	5.13
Tempest	42	25	3.00	1.79	4.79

For somewhere about three-fourths of Shakespeare's dramatic career there are very few light endings, and only a trace of weak endings. They furnish no chronological hints until we come to about the year 1606, but they are a "very sensitive indicator of Shakespeare's latest manner".[2] A wide gap separates the light endings of *Macbeth* from those of all previous plays

[1] From Ingram's Table (*T. N. S. S.* 1874, p. 450). The percentages will be found to differ slightly from Ingram's because he counted in the pentameter rimed lines (See p. 449), as well as blank verse, thus confusing two tests. "Rimes and weak endings are incompatible," emphatic syllables being necessary in the riming words. (Fleay in Ingleby, p. 60, Rule 3).

[2] So Ingram, p. 455. But I cannot agree with Dowden (*Primer*, p. 41) that within the last period this test "serves to indicate nearly the precise order in which the plays were written."

(twenty-one as against eleven in *All's Well*, the highest figure preceding). *Macbeth* thus prepares the way for the Weak-Ending Period, and was, in all probability, the last play written before it. With this mild forewarning, the poet seems to have thrown himself at once, and whole-heartedly, into the practice of light and weak endings. Twenty-eight of the latter appear in *Antony and Cleopatra*, forty-four in *Coriolanus*, fifty-two in *Cymbeline*, while the light endings leap to seventy-one in *Antony and Cleopatra*, sixty in *Coriolanus*, seventy-eight in *Cymbeline*. No play before *Macbeth* shows more than two weak endings. This, I take it, is by all odds the most important piece of metrical testimony in regard to the date of *Macbeth*. On the one hand, the comparatively large number of light endings indicates emphatically that the play was written after *Hamlet*, *Othello*, and *Lear*. On the other hand, the theory of a late date for *Macbeth* (about 1610) is conclusively controverted by the absolutely small number of weak endings and the relatively small number of light endings, as compared with *Antony and Cleopatra*, *Coriolanus*, *Cymbeline*, *The Winter's Tale*, and *The Tempest*. These metrical statistics alone, unaided by the evidence of style, Shakespeare's dramatic mood, etc., are enough to prove that *Macbeth* cannot belong in the same period as the Romances.[1]

Commonly a pause occurs either shortly or immediately before the final monosyllable, in these light and weak endings, after which the verse darts ahead.

[1] See Verity, pp. x, xi. In the case of light and weak endings, as in connection with ordinary run-on lines, one should note the use of the peculiarity in *successive* lines. Before *Macbeth* occurrences are always solitary. But *upon* comes at the end of ll. 69 and 70 in I. 7, and instances of two and three in succession begin to be frequent in *Antony and Cleopatra*. See König, pp. 106-108.

But fear not yet
To take upon you what is yours : ‖ you may
Convey your pleasures in a spacious plenty. (IV. 3.70).

The latter part of a line, if it is to be bound into a rhythmical unit with the next, must not be too long; and so an increase in the number of *enjambements* is accompanied by a shoving back of the cæsura toward the end of the line. This structure, as Craik[1] has well said, conduces to variety and liveliness, and is better fitted for the sprightly, varicoloured portrayal of life which we have in the Romances than for the massy weight of the great tragedies. The "manner of its gait" is like Diomed's:—

He rises on the toe: that spirit of his
In aspiration lifts him from the earth.
(*Troilus and Cressida*, IV. 5.15, 16)

TABLE OF CÆSURAS.[2]

Play	After 1st, 2nd, or 3rd Syllable	Regular Place After 4th, or 5th Syllable	After 6th, 7th, 8th, or 9th Syllable
Comedy of Errors. . .	150	526	295
Merchant of Venice .	109	520	339
Henry V.	141	466	334
Macbeth	56	380	527

F. Speech Endings.

The last test to be considered is the Speech-Ending Test.[3] It is really a corollary or buttress of the *enjambement*-test. As Shakespeare composed less and less within the bounds of the single line, and more and more in rhythmical phrases, and as these phrases came to a conclusion at the cæsura, and not at the end of the

[1] P. 36.

[2] From Conrad's Table in *Jahrbuch* XXXI., p. 347, based on a thousand lines in each play.

[3] Proposed by Ingram, worked out for twenty plays by Prof. Pulling (*T. N. S. S.* 1877-1879, p. 457), and for all the dramas by König (p. 134).

verse, so also the speeches of the characters ended increasingly within the line. The broken structure removes from the dialogue much of that air of artificiality which attaches to the poetic drama. This is well illustrated by Act V., Scene 4:—

Malcolm. Cousins, I hope the days are near at hand
That chambers will be safe.
Menteith. We doubt it nothing.
Siward. What wood is this before us?
Menteith. The wood of Birnam.
Malcolm. Let every soldier hew him down a bough
And bear 't before him: thereby shall we shadow
The numbers of our host, and make discovery
Err in report of us?
Soldiers. It shall be done.
Siward. We learn no other but the confident tyrant
Keeps still in Dunsinane, and will endure
Our setting down before 't.
Malcolm. 'Tis his main hope:
For where there is advantage to be given,
Both more and less have given him the revolt,
And none serve with him but constrained things
Whose hearts are absent too.
Macduff. Let our just censures
Attend the true event, and put we on
Industrious soldiership.
Siward. The time approaches
That will with due decision make us know
What we shall say we have and what we owe.
Thoughts speculative their unsure hopes relate,
But certain issue strokes must arbitrate:
Towards which advance the war.

The speech-ending test, though interesting and suggestive, is of comparatively little importance as strict evidence, because the materials are inadequate.[1]

[1] That is to say, the total number of speech endings is not great enough for small differences in percentages in the several plays to indicate anything in regard to order of composition. See König, p. 134.

As far as it goes, it seems to place *Macbeth* nearer to *Antony and Cleopatra* than to *Lear*.

TABLE OF SPEECH ENDINGS.[1]

Play	Per Cent. of Blank Verse Speeches Ending in Middle of Line	Per Cent. of Verse Speeches Ending in Middle of Line	Total Number of Speeches Ending in Middle of Line	Two Speeches in One Line	Three Speeches	Four Speeches
Love's Labour's Lost	10.	?	?			
Comedy of Errors .	.6	1.23	6	10	1	0
Merchant of Venice .	22.2	17.03	79	33	0	0
Henry V.	18.3	16.09	43	18	0	0
Hamlet	51.6	30.19	205			
Othello	41.4	26.1	245			
Lear	60.9	39.08	290			
Macbeth	77.2	40.44	239	127	4	1
Ant. and Cleo. . . .	77.5	?	?			
Winter's Tale . . .	87.6	66.93	340			
Tempest	84.5	61.86	253			

IV. Summary.

It is convenient to divide Shakespeare's dramatic career, as far as it concerns metre, into four parts, to which, after the manner of Dowden, we may apply certain fanciful catch-words.

Period I. The Vanity of Rime. This period is characterized saliently by its large amount of rime, with the attendant trickeries of alternates, sonnets, and doggerels. The number of run-on lines, of feminine endings, of Alexandrines, and of speeches ending within the line, is very small.[2] There are practically no feminine mid-line syllables, practically no light or weak

[1] The first column is from König, p. 134; it is decidedly more reliable and intelligent than columns two and three, which are from Pulling's Tables, because it does not include rimed and one-line speeches in reckoning the percentage. The last three columns are from *Jahrbuch*, XXXI. p. 340, and show how Shakespeare's habit increased of dividing one line among several speeches.

[2] *Cf.* Fleay, *Manual*, pp. 131-133, and Schipper, II. i., 296.

endings. This period extends to 1594; in it fall *Love's Labour's Lost*, *The Comedy of Errors*, *The Two Gentlemen of Verona*, *A Midsummer-Night's Dream*, and *Richard III.*,[1] the last lacking in rime, but belonging here by every other characteristic.

On the border-line between this group and the next is *Richard II.*

As a typical example of an early passage in metre I select *Love's Labour's Lost*, I. 1.33-64.

Biron. I can but say their protestation over;
So much, dear liege, I have already sworn,
That is, to live and study here three years.
But there are other strict observances;
As, not to see a woman in that term,
Which I hope well is not enrolled there;
And one day in a week to touch no food
And but one meal on every day beside,
The which I hope is not enrolled there;
And then, to sleep but three hours in the night,
And not be seen to wink of all the day—
When I was wont to think no harm all night
And make a dark night too of half the day—
Which I hope well is not enrolled there:
O, these are barren tasks, too hard to keep,
Not to see ladies, study, fast, not sleep!
King. Your oath is pass'd to pass away from these.
Biron. Let me say no, my liege, an if you please:
I only swore to study with your grace
And stay here in your court for three years' space.
Longaville. You swore to that, Biron, and to the rest.
Biron. By yea and nay, sir, then I swore in jest.
What is the end of study? let me know.

[1] For the sake of simplicity I avoid in this discussion those plays the date of composition of which is not fixed, probably because they underwent revision in different periods of authorship, *viz.*, *Romeo and Juliet*, *All's Well*, and *Troilus and Cressida*, and those in which another hand than Shakespeare's is to be discerned, *viz.*, *The Taming of the Shrew*, 1, 2, and 3 *Henry VI.*, *Henry VIII.*, *Titus Andronicus*, *Timon*, *and Pericles.*

King. Why, that to know, which else we should not know.
Biron. Things hid and barr'd, you mean, from common sense?
King. Ay, that is study's god-like recompense.
Biron. Come on, then; I will swear to study so,
To know the thing I am forbid to know:
As thus,—to study where I well may dine,
When I to feast expressly am forbid;
Or study where to meet some mistress fine,
When mistresses from common sense are hid.

Period II. The Balance of Power. This period is distinguished from the preceding mainly by the diminution of riming lines. Prose becomes a vital part of the Histories. *Enjambement*, double endings, cæsural syllables, and broken speeches increase, but are still insignificant. Alexandrines and short lines continue few, and light and weak endings are almost undiscoverable. The close of this period marks Shakespeare's most even and easy balance of thought and metre. The verse's internal structure is at the perfection of its melody, and the normal foot and normal line are returned to often enough to be felt as the units of composition. *King John*, *The Merchant of Venice*, 1 and 2 *Henry IV.*, *The Merry Wives of Windsor*, *Henry V.*, *Much Ado About Nothing*, *As You Like It*, *Twelfth Night* and *Julius Caesar* (1591–1601) are here included. The last shows some of the qualities of the Third Period.

The famous soliloquy of the King, from 2 *Henry IV.*, III. 1.4-31, will serve as a characteristic instance:—

How many thousands of my poorest subjects
Are at this hour asleep! O sleep, O gentle sleep,
Nature's soft nurse, how have I frighted thee,
That thou no more wilt weigh my eyelids down
And steep my senses in forgetfulness?
Why rather, sleep, liest thou in smoky cribs,
Upon uneasy pallets stretching thee
And hush'd with buzzing night-flies to thy slumber,
Than in the perfumed chambers of the great,

Under the canopies of costly state,
And lull'd with sound of sweetest melody?
O thou dull god, why liest thou with the vile
In loathsome beds, and leavest the kingly couch
A watch-case or a common 'larum-bell?
Wilt thou upon the high and giddy mast
Seal up the ship-boy's eyes, and rock his brains
In cradle of the rude imperious surge
And in the visitation of the winds,
Who take the ruffian billows by the top,
Curling their monstrous heads and hanging them
With deafening clamour in the slippery clouds,
That, with the hurly, death itself awakes?
Canst thou, O partial sleep, give thy repose
To the wet sea-boy in an hour so rude,
And in the calmest and most stillest night,
With all appliances and means to boot,
Deny it to a king? Then happy low, lie down!
Uneasy lies the head that wears a crown.

Period III. The Discordant Weight of Thought. This period is far removed from its predecessor in the matter of Alexandrines and short lines, mid-line-ending speeches, and mid-line feminine syllables. The use of prose becomes wider and wider in range.[1] *Enjambement* and feminine endings pursue their broken progress up the scale. Rime remains on a low level. Light and weak endings are still very infrequent. This period is short (1603-1605), but in it were written the world's greatest romantic tragedies, *Hamlet*, *Othello*, *Lear*, with the great tragi-comedy, *Measure for Measure*, and the burden of the tragic themes is almost more than the metre can uphold. The poet begins to find that his packed eagerness of thought and feverish excitement of passion are at odds with mere harmony and grace.

[1] On the development of prose in this and the following period see the admirable chapter by Seccombe and Allen, in *The Age of Shakespeare*, vol. II., pp. 117 ff. See also Janssen, *passim*.

I take part of the scene between Hamlet and his mother as an illustration (*Hamlet*, III. 4.68-102).

Hamlet. You cannot call it love; for at your age
The hey-day in the blood is tame, it's humble,
And waits upon the judgement: and what judgement
Would step from this to this? Sense, sure, you have,
Else could you not have motion; but sure, that sense
Is apoplex'd; for madness would not err,
Nor sense to ecstasy was ne'er so thrall'd
But it reserved some quantity of choice,
To serve in such a difference. What devil was't
That thus hath cozen'd you at hoodman-blind?
Eyes without feeling, feeling without sight,
Ears without hands or eyes, smelling sans all,
Or but a sickly part of one true sense
Could not so mope.
O shame! where is thy blush? Rebellious hell,
If thou canst mutine in a matron's bones,
To flaming youth let virtue be as wax,
And melt in her own fire: proclaim no shame
When the compulsive ardour gives the charge,
Since frost itself as actively doth burn
And reason pandars will.

Queen. O Hamlet, speak no more
Thou turn'st mine eyes into my very soul;
And there I see such black and grained spots,
As will not leave their tinct.

Hamlet. Nay, but to live
In the rank sweat of an enseamed bed,
Stew'd in corruption, honeying and making love
Over the nasty sty,—

Queen. O, speak to me no more;
These words, like daggers, enter in mine ears;
No more, sweet Hamlet!

Hamlet. A murderer and a villain;
A slave that is not twentieth part the tithe
Of your precedent lord; a vice of kings;
A cutpurse of the empire and the rule,
That from a shelf the precious diadem stole,
And put it in his pocket!

Queen. No more!
Hamlet. A king of shreds and patches.

Period IV. The License of Weak Endings. The general carelessness of art which stamps Shakespeare's final period (1607–1612) confronts us most strikingly in a great crowd of light and weak endings, and only less so in the climax of run-on lines and feminine endings. Rime has all but vanished. Alexandrines and short lines seem, if anything, to recede, but there is no other evidence to support Mr. Fleay,[1] who surmises that *Antony and Cleopatra*, *Coriolanus*, *Cymbeline*, *The Winter's Tale*, and *The Tempest* were produced at greater leisure, and more carefully polished. Rather let us say that the return to Stratford cast upon Shakespeare the weight of too much liberty. The poetry is so licentious that it is often difficult to distinguish from the chartered libertine, prose.[2]

The dialogue between the Queen and Cornelius in *Cymbeline* (I. 5.6-42) will serve as a typical example of the metre of this period, all the more typical perhaps because it is in no sense a "purple" passage.

Cornelius. [*Presenting a small box.*
But I beseech your grace, without offence,—
My conscience bids me ask—wherefore you have

[1] *Manual*, p. 133.

[2] Seccombe and Allen (II., p. 114) print *Coriolanus*, II. 2.86-96 as prose and very justly say, "Written thus this passage is not quite obviously verse, and it would be possible for a dull ear to miss its cadences in reading." Of *Cymbeline*, Professor Barrett Wendell says (*William Shakspere*, p. 357), "Endstopped lines are so deliberately avoided that one feels a sense of relief when a speech and a line end together. Such a phrase as 'How slow his soul sail'd on, how swift his ship' is deliberately made, not a single line, but two half-lines. Several times, in the broken dialogue, one has literally to count the syllables before the metrical regularity of the verse appears. . . . Clearly this puzzling style is decadent; the distinction between verse and prose is breaking down."

Commanded of me these most poisonous compounds,
Which are the movers of a languishing death;
But though slow, deadly?

Queen. I wonder, doctor,
Thou ask'st me such a question. Have I not been
Thy pupil long? Hast thou not learn'd me how
To make perfumes? distil? preserve? yea, so
That our great king himself doth woo me oft
For my confections? Having thus far proceeded,—
Unless thou think'st me devilish—is't not meet
That I did amplify my judgement in
Other conclusions? I will try the forces
Of these thy compounds on such creatures as
We count not worth the hanging, but none human,
To try the vigour of them and apply
Allayments to their act, and by them gather
Their several virtues and effects.

Cornelius. Your highness
Shall from this practice but make hard your heart:
Besides, the seeing these effects will be
Both noisome and infectious.

Queen. O, content thee.

Enter Pisanio.

[*Aside*] Here comes a flattering rascal; upon him
Will I first work; he's for his master,
And enemy to my son. How now, Pisanio!
Doctor, your service for the time is ended;
Take your own way.

Cornelius. [*Aside*] I do suspect you madam:
But you shall do no harm.

Queen. [*To Pisanio*] Hark thee, a word.

Cornelius. [*Aside*] I do not like her. She doth think she has
Strange lingering poisons: I do not know her spirit
And will not trust one of her malice with
A drug of such damn'd nature. Those she has
Will stupefy and dull the sense awhile;
Which first, perchance, she'll prove on cats and dogs,
Then afterward up higher: but there is
No danger in what show of death it makes,
More than the locking-up the spirits a time,
To be more fresh, reviving.

Between the last two periods *Macbeth* is to be placed in a sort of dependent isolation, belonging in the Third by most of its features, but pointing to the Fourth with its generous total of light endings.

APPENDIX

By way of Explanation and Addition.

p. 7, footnote 3. Prose in History was familiar to Shakespeare by his work as a reviser of 2 *Henry VI.*, where it appears in I. 1, 3, 4; II. 1, 3; IV. 2, 3, 6, 7, 8, 10, and is notable in the humourous Jack Cade scenes. It is rather curious that when it began to write alone in *Richard III.*, *Richard II.*, and *King John*, he did not turn to it for comic relief.

p. 19, footnote 3. Add to the list of rimed pentameter lines III. 5. 12, 21, which are in the midst of Hecate's tetrameters.

p. 35. Add to the list of participles in which the *e* of the ending is sounded: *damnèd* (I. 2.14); *damnèd* (III. 6. 10); *charmèd* (IV. 1.9); *charmèd* (V. 8.12.)

p. 36. The M. E. form of *captain* was *capitain*, adopted from late O. F. (14th C.) *capitaine*. *The New English Dictionary* cites examples of spelling with an *i* or *y* as late as 1567. Probably the word was still frequently pronounced as a trisyllable in Shakespeare's time. *Cf.* 3 *Henry VI.*, IV. 7.30, "A wise stout captain, and soon persuaded." The French word *capitaine* is used by Shakespeare in *Henry V.*, IV. 4.70.

TABLES FOR TWENTY-SIX PLAYS.

Play	Total Lines	Lines of Prose	Lines of Blank Verse	Per Cent. of Rimed Heroics in Verse Lines	Number of Alternates	Number of Alexandrines	Number of Short Lines	Per Cent. of Feminine Endings	Number of Feminine Mid-Line Syllables	Per Cent. of Run-on Lines	Number of Light Endings	Number of Weak Endings	Per Cent. of Mid-Line-Ending Speeches	Conjectural Date
Love's Labour's Lost...	2785	1022	617	62.2	242	4	23	7.7	0	18.4	3	0	10.0	1590
Comedy of Errors.......	1777	226	1156	19.4	64	8	17	16.6	0	12.9	0	0	.6	1591
Two Gentlemen..........	2292	659	1431	6.5	19	16	74	18.4	5	12.4	0	0	5.8	1592–1593
Mid. Night's Dream...	2166	493	729	43.4	96	0	24	7.3	1	13.2	0	1	17.3	1593–1594
Richard III (F)...........	3589	63	3278	3.5	0	?	96	19.5	11	13.1	4	0	2.9	1593
Richard II..................	2756	0	2174	18.6	4	53?	73	11.0	18	19.9	4	0	7.3	1594
King John..................	2570	0	2403	4.5	12	5	18	6.3	?	17.7	7	0	12.1	1595
Merchant of Venice.....	2656	604	1872	4.6	4	12	46	17.7	32	21.5	6	1	22.2	1594–1596
1 Henry IV................	3176	1464	1561	2.7	4	6	65	5.1	19	22.8	5	2	14.2	1597
2 Henry IV..............	3446	1857	1425	2.9	0	7	31	16.3	21	21.4	1	0	16.8	1598
Merry Wives (F).........	3029	2676	207	6.4	0	3	7	27.2	8	20.1	1	0	20.5	1598
Henry V....................	3559	1367	1918	3.2	0	12	31	20.5	25	21.8	2	0	18.3	1599
Much Ado..................	2825	2105	618	5.2	22	5	26	22.9	11	19.3	1	1	20.7	1599
As You Like It...........	2839	1679	871	6.3	10	8	42	25.5	22	17.1	2	0	21.6	1599
Twelfth Night	2690	1731	724	13.7	0	6	59	25.6	28	14.7	3	1	36.3	1600
Julius Caesar.............	2477	156	2181	1.2	0	21	108	19.7	35	19.3	10	0	20.3	1601
Measure for Measure..	2810	1134	1470	3.6	0	60	117	26.1	98	23.0	7	0	51.4	1603
Hamlet	3929	1200	2358	2.7	0	43	158	22.6	78	23.1	8	0	51.6	1603
Othello	3316	661	2381	3.2	0	66	171	28 1	208	19.5	2	0	41.4	1604
Lear	3328	896	2072	3.4	0	60	191	28.5	131	29.3	5	1	60.9	1605
Macbeth	2106	158	1611	5.8	0	28	97	26.3	78	36.6	21	2	77.2	1606
Ant. and Cleo.............	3059	287	2589	.7	0	39	143	26.5	120	43.3	71	28	77.5	1607
Coriolanus.................	3406	829	2413	.9	0	41	136	28.4	120	45.9	60	44	79.0	1608
Cymbeline..................	3339	535	2528	3.2	23	38	68	30.7	90	46.0	78	52	85.0	1609
Winter's Tale............	3074	979	1948	.0	0	56?	58	32.9	60	37.5	57	43	87.6	1610–1612
Tempest.....................	2062	458	1396	.1	0	15	70	35.4	33	41.5	42	25	84.5	1610–1611

BIBLIOGRAPHY

Of books and articles used and referred to.

The references to the text of Shakespeare are to the Globe Edition ; of Middleton, to Bullen's Edition in eight volumes.

EDITIONS OF MACBETH :—

Clarendon Press : W. G. Clark and W. A. Wright : pp. x, xi.

Arden : E. K. Chambers : Appendix on Metre.

Pitt Press : A. W. Verity : Introduction, and Appendix on Metre.

Longmans' English Classics : J. M. Manly : pp. xxxii–xxxv.

Leopold : F. J. Furnivall : pp. xix, xx, cxxiii.

Variorum : H. H. Furness : pp. 259, 303.

Eversley : C. H. Herford : Introduction.

Elizabethan : Mark H. Liddell : p. 165.

WORKS IN ENGLISH :—

CHARLES BATHURST : *Remarks on the Differences in Shakespeare's Versification in Different Periods of his Life.*

GEORGE L. CRAIK : *The English of Shakespeare :* pp. 28–43.

WILLIAM SIDNEY WALKER : *Shakespeare's Versification :* p. 227.

E. A. ABBOTT : *A Shakespearean Grammar :* pp. 328–429.

FREDERICK GARD FLEAY : *Shakespeare Manual :* pp. 121–138, 239–261.

FREDERICK GARD FLEAY : *Introduction to Shakespearean Study :* p. 36.

FREDERICK GARD FLEAY : *Life and Work of Shakespeare :* p, 239.

C. M. INGLEBY : *Shakespeare, The Man and the Book :* Vol. II., ch. II., pp. 40–49 ; also ch. III., pp. 50–141, by F. G. FLEAY.

EDWARD DOWDEN : *Shakspere Primer :* pp. 39–46.

HIRAM CORSON : *Introduction to Shakespeare :* pp. 51–82.

JOHN ADDINGTON SYMONDS : *Blank Verse :* Section II., "The History of Blank Verse".

JOSEPH B. MAYOR : *Chapters on English Metre :* pp. 146–183.

THOMAS SECCOMBE AND J. W. ALLEN : *The Age of Shakespere :* Vol. II., pp. 111–122.

GEORGE H. BROWNE : *Notes on Shakspere's Versification :* pp. 9, 21.

RAYMOND M. ALDEN : *English Verse :* pp. 55, 184 ff., 226, 437 ff.

FRANCIS B. GUMMERE : *Handbook of Poetics :* p. 142.

ALEXANDER SCHMIDT : *Shakespeare Lexicon :* Vol. II., p. 1413.

HALLAM TENNYSON : *Alfred, Lord Tennyson, A Memoir :* Vol. II., p. 14.

G. C. MACAULAY : *Francis Beaumont :* pp. 43, 44.

BARRETT WENDELL : *William Shakspere :* p. 357.

ENGLISH ARTICLES IN PERIODICALS :—

Transactions of the New Shakspere Society 1874–75 : passim ; especially the discussion on Fleay's First Paper (pp. 17–37) and the article by J. K. Ingram "On the 'Weak Endings of Shakspere'" (pp. 442–464).

The same, 1877–79, pp. 457, 458 : F. S. Pulling : "The 'Speech-Ending Test' Applied to Twenty of Shakspere's Plays."

The same, 1880–6, pp. 523–562 : Henry Sharpe : "The Prose in Shakpere's Plays."

Englische Studien : Band III., pp. 473–503 : J. Harrison, J. Goodlet and R. Boyle : "Report of the Tests Committee of the St. Petersburg Shakespeare Circle."

Transactions of the Philological Society, June 1876 : article by A. J. Ellis.

WORKS IN GERMAN :—

GOSWIN KÖNIG : *Der Vers in Shaksperes Dramen : passim.*

J. SCHIPPER : *Englische Metrik,* II., i., pp. 287–316.

V. F. JANSSEN : *Die Prosa in Shakespeares Dramen : passim.*

GERMAN ARTICLES IN PERIODICALS :—

Jahrbuch der Deutchen Shakespeare-Gesellschaft, Vol. V., pp. 227–273 : N. Delius : "Die Prosa in Shakespeare's Dramen."

The same, XIII., pp. 248–266: W. Hertzberg: "Metrisches, Grammatisches, Chronologisches zu Shakespeares Dramen."

The same, XXVIII., pp. 177–272: Julius Heuser: "Der Coupletreim in Shakespeares Dramen."

The same, XXXI, pp. 318–353: Hermann Conrad: "Metrische Untersuchungen zur Feststellung der Abfassungszeit von Shakespeares Dramen."

Anglia, XIII, pp. 353–357: A. Wagner: "Metrische Bemerkungen zu Shakespeares Macbeth".